CHRIST OUR LIGHT

PRAYING THE TRIDUUM

CHRIST OUR LIGHT

ASSEMBLY EDITION

WORLD LIBRARY PUBLICATIONS
3825 N. Willow Road
Schiller Park, Illinois 60176

This resource was edited by Jerry Galipeau and Alan J. Hommerding.
Original artwork is by Suzanne Novak and the design is by Kathy Ade and Chris Myers.

With Ecclesiastical Approbation

CONTENTS

HOLY THURSDAY

$\mathcal{H}$OLY $\mathcal{T}$HURSDAY

EVENING MASS
OF THE
LORD'S SUPPER

"We should glory in the cross of our Lord Jesus Christ, for he is our salvation, our life and resurrection; through him we are saved and made free."

This entrance antiphon for Holy Thursday's Evening Mass of the Lord's Supper announces the intention of the Sacred Triduum. During the Triduum, these sacred "three days," God gathers us together to remember the events that constitute the paschal mystery of our Savior Jesus Christ: his life, passion, death, and resurrection. We who are Christian remember that in baptism we entered into the paschal mystery: we died to sin and rose to new life with Christ. We who are preparing for baptism enter these days surrounded by signs and symbols that will plunge us into the paschal mystery.

As we begin this Sacred Triduum, we carry the holy oils blessed by our bishop at this week's Chrism Mass. Oil of the Catechumens, Oil of the Sick, and Sacred Chrism are solemnly presented. These oils will be used throughout the year to anoint the sick, those preparing for Baptism, the newly baptized, and those being confirmed.

In tonight's proclamation of God's word, we begin by remembering the Passover, the remarkable event that inaugurated the Israelites' release from their Egyptian captors. Set against the backdrop of this Passover, we remember the new Passover, the Eucharist, celebrated by Christ and his friends. Tonight we hear the account of the Last Supper from John's gospel. In solemn remembrance, we do what Jesus commanded: we wash feet. Washing feet is a sign of the humble service to which Christians are called. To be people of the Eucharist is to be foot-washers. The Lord is clear: his very body and blood consumed here must transform and strengthen us for service to the poor.

We celebrate Eucharist on this sacred night. Following the sharing of communion, the sacred Body of Christ is taken, in solemn procession, to its place of repose. We are called to spend time in prayer with the Lord. This Sacred Triduum has begun, making us open and vulnerable to God's action in our lives throughout the holy moments of these three days. We stand at the threshold between our forty-day celebration of Lent and the Sacred Triduum. Let us enter these days with hearts open to God's action, for this is a true moment of grace.

HOLY THURSDAY

EVENING MASS
OF THE
LORD'S SUPPER

Hymn

Lift high the cross, the love of Christ pro - claim, Till

all the world___ a - dore___ his sa - cred name.

1. Come, Chris-tians, fol - low where our Sav - ior trod, Our
2. Led on their way by this tri - um-phant sign, The
3. All new - born fol - l'wers of the Cru - ci - fied Bear
4. O Lord, once lift - ed on the glo - ri-ous tree, As
5. So shall our song of tri - umph ev - er be: Praise

D.C.

1. King vic - to - ri-ous, Christ, the Son of God.
2. hosts of___ God in glo - ri-ous ranks com - bine.
3. on their___ brows the seal of him who died.
4. you have___ prom - ised, save and set us free.
5. to the___ Cru - ci - fied for vic - to - ry!

George W. Kitchin, 1827–1912, alt.
Michael R. Newbolt, 1874–1956, alt.

Sydney H. Nicholson, 1875–1947
Text and music © 1974, Hope Publishing Co.

The Reception of the Holy Oils
Blessed at the Chrism Mass

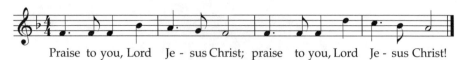

Praise to you, Lord Je - sus Christ; praise to you, Lord Je - sus Christ!

Paul Inwood
Music © 1996, Paul Inwood

Penitential Rite

Gloria

Glo - ry to God in the high - est, _____ and

peace to his peo - ple on earth. _____

Howard L. Hughes
Music © 1990, WLP

Liturgy of the Word

First Reading *Exodus 12:1–8, 11–14*

Responsorial Psalm *Psalm 116:12–13, 15–16bc, 17–18*

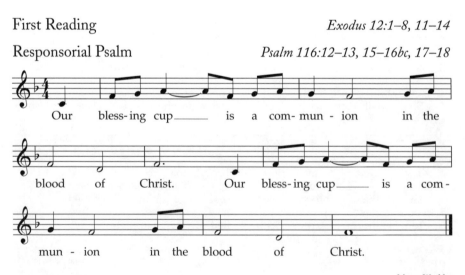

Our bless-ing cup _____ is a com- mun - ion in the

blood of Christ. Our bless-ing cup _____ is a com -

mun - ion in the blood of Christ.

Text © 1969, ICEL

Marcy Weckler
Music © 1993, WLP

Second Reading

1 Corinthians 11:23–26

Gospel Acclamation

R/. Praise and hon-or to you, Lord Je-sus Christ! Christ!

Music © 1994, WLP

Paul M. French

Gospel

John 13:1–15

Homily

Washing of Feet

Je - su,____ Je - su,____ fill us with your love, show

us how to serve the neigh-bors we have from you.

1. Kneels at the feet of his friends,
2. Neigh - bors are rich____ and poor,
3. These are the ones we should serve,
4. Kneel at the feet of our friends,

1. Si - lent - ly wash - es their feet,
2. Neigh - bors are black____ and white,
3. These are the ones we should love.
4. Si - lent - ly wash - ing their feet,

D.C.

1. Mas - ter who pours out him - self____ for them.____
2. Neigh-bors are near____ and far____ a - way.____
3. All____ are neigh-bors to us____ and you.____
4. This is the way we should live____ with you.____

Tr. by Tom Colvin

Ghana folk song
Adapt. by Tom Colvin
Tr. and adapt. © 1969, 1982, Hope Publishing Co.

– or –

When - ev - er you serve me, says the Lord, my Fa - ther in heav-en will hon-or you. When - ev- er you serve me, says the Lord, my Fa - ther will hon - or you.

Steven R. Janco
Text and music © 1995, WLP

Dismissal of the Elect and Catechumens

General Intercessions

Lord, hear our prayer; De - us, ex - au - di nos; Se - ñor, es - cú - cha - nos.

Mike Hay (1953–1999)
Music © 1994, WLP

Liturgy of the Eucharist

Preparation of the Gifts

1. Where char - i - ty and love pre - vail,
2. With grate - ful joy and ho - ly fear
3. For - give we now each oth - er's faults

4. Let strife a - mong us be un - known,
5. Let us re - call that in our midst
6. No race nor creed can love ex - clude

1. There God is ev - er found; Brought here to - geth - er
2. God's char - i - ty we learn; Let us with heart and
3. As we our faults con - fess; And let us love each

4. Let all con - ten - tion cease; Be God's the glo - ry
5. Dwells God's be - got - ten Son; As mem - bers of his
6. If hon - ored be God's name; Our fam - i - ly em -

1. by Christ's love, By love are we thus bound.
2. mind and soul Now love God in re - turn.
3. oth - er well In Chris - tian ho - li - ness.

4. that we seek, Be ours God's ho - ly peace.
5. bod - y joined, We are in Christ made one.
6. brac - es all Whose Fa - ther is the same.

Based on *Ubi caritas*, 9th cent.
Omer Westendorf

Paul Benoit, 1893–1979
Text and music © 1960, WLP

Eucharistic Prayer

Preface Acclamation

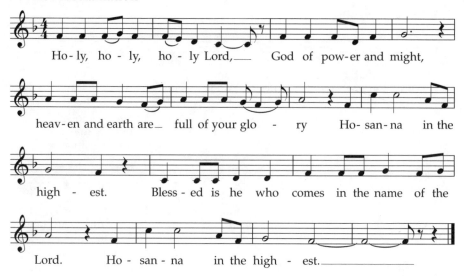

Ho-ly, ho-ly, ho-ly Lord,— God of pow-er and might, heav-en and earth are— full of your glo - ry Ho-san-na in the high - est. Bless-ed is he who comes in the name of the Lord. Ho - san - na in the high - est.

People's Mass
Jan M. Vermulst, 1925–1994
Music © 1970, 1984, WLP

Memorial Acclamation

Christ has died, Christ is ris - en, Christ will come a - gain.

Great Amen

A - men. A - men. A - men.

Danish Amen Mass
David Kraehenbuehl, 1923–1997
Music © 1970, 1973, WLP

Communion Rite

Lord's Prayer

Sign of Peace

Lamb of God

A-gnus De - i, qui tol- lis pec-cá- ta mun-di: mi-se-ré-re no - bis.

A-gnus De - i, qui tol- lis pec-cá- ta mun-di: mi-se-ré-re no - bis.

A-gnus De - i, qui tol- lis pec-cá- ta mun-di: do-na no-bis pa - cem.

Jubilate Deo
Mass XVIII, Chant

Communion Procession

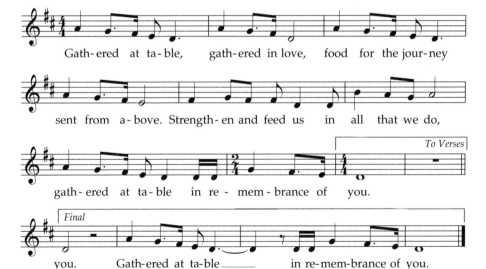

Gath-ered at ta- ble, gath-ered in love, food for the jour-ney

sent from a-bove. Strength-en and feed us in all that we do,

To Verses

gath-ered at ta-ble in re - mem-brance of you.

Final

you. Gath-ered at ta-ble_____ in re-mem-brance of you.

Paul A. Tate
Text and music © 1997, WLP

Transfer of the Holy Eucharist

1. Praise we Christ's im - mor - tal bod - y, And_ his pre - cious
2. Com - ing forth from spot-less Maid - en He_ for us was
3. On the eve of_ that last sup - per, Break - ing bread with

1. *Pan - ge, lin - gua,_ glo - ri - ó - si Cór - po - ris my -*
2. *No - bis da - tus,_ no - bis na - tus Ex_ in - tá - cta*
3. *In su - pré - mae_ noc - te coe - nae, Re - cúm - bens cum*

1. blood we praise;_ Born of roy - al Vir - gin Moth - er,
2. born a man!_ Sow - ing seeds of truth a - mong us,
3. cho - sen friends,_ He o - beys the Law's di - rec - tions

1. *sté - ri - um,_ San - gui - nís - que pre - ti - ó - si,*
2. *Vír - gi - ne,_ Et in mun - do con - ver - sá - tus,*
3. *frá - tri - bus,_ Ob - ser - vá - ta le - ge ple - ne*

1. He shall reign for end - less days!_ Dy - ing once to save
2. He ful - filled the Fa - ther's plan;_ Then his fi - nal night
3. E - ven as the old Law ends._ Now he hands the Twelve

1. *Quem in mun - di pré - ti - um._ Fruc - tus ven - tris ge -*
2. *Spar - so ver - bi sé - mi - ne,_ Su - i mo - ras in -*
3. *Ci - bis in le - gá - li - bus,_ Ci - bum tur - bae du -*

1. all na - tions, Ev - er - more he_ wins our praise!
2. up - on him, Won - drous - ly that_ night be - gan!
3. a new bread; His own flesh with their flesh blends! A - men._

1. *ne - ró - si Rex ef - fú - dit_ gén - ti - um.*
2. *co - lá - tus Mi - ro clau - sit_ ór - di - ne.*
3. *o - dé - nae Se dat su - is_ má - ni - bus. A - men.*

4. By a word, the Word embodied
Changes common bread and wine;
Bread becomes his holy body,
Wine is made his blood divine!
Though this truth evades the senses,
Faith unveils the sacred sign!

4. *Verbum caro, panem verum*
Verbo carnum éfficit:
Fitque sanguis Christi merum,
Et si sensus déficit
Ad firmándum cor sincérum
Sola fides súfficit.

5. Humbly let us voice our homage
   For so great a sacrament;
   Let all former rites surrender
   To the Lord's New Testament;
   What our senses fail to fathom,
   Let us grasp through faith's consent!

6. Glory, honor, adoration
   Let us sing with one accord!
   Praised be God, almighty Father;
   Praised be Christ, his Son, our Lord;
   Praised be God the Holy Spirit;
   Triune Godhead be adored! Amen.

5. *Tantum ergo Sacraméntum*
   Venerémur cérnui:
   Et antíquum documéntum
   Novo cedat rítui:
   Praestet fides suppleméntum
   Sénsuum deféctui.

6. *Genitóri, Genitóque*
   Laus et jubilátio,
   Salus, honor, virtus quoque
   Sit et benedíctio:
   Procedénti ab utróque
   Compar sit laudátio. Amen.

Thomas Aquinas, c. 1227–1274, alt.
Tr. by Melvin Farrell, 1930–1986
Tr. © 1964, WLP

HOLY THURSDAY
PRAYER DURING THE NIGHT WATCH

Gathering

Ag - nus De - i, mi - se - re - re no - bis.
or: Ho - ly Lamb of God, in your mer - cy, hear— us.

Alan J. Hommerding
Text (English) and music © 1994, WLP

Prayer

Psalmody

Psalm 134

Si - lent- ly, peace- ful- ly, we will rest in you.

Mike Hay (1953–1999)
Text and music © 1993, WLP

Reading

Hebrews 13:12–15

Responsory

Stay with us, Lord Jesus Christ, for night has come.

Lk 24:29

Lucien Deiss
Text and music © 1995, WLP

Canticle of Simeon

1. In peace, dismiss your servant, Lord, Your
2. A glorious light has been revealed In
3. Give glory to our God on high, To

1. vow to me has been fulfilled; My eyes have seen the
2. love, to shine in ev-'ry land: The pride of chosen
3. Jesus Christ all glory raise, And glory to the

1. saving grace, Your promise for all nations willed.
2. Israel, Made manifest by your own hand.
3. Spirit sing In never-ending thanks and praise.

Alan J. Hommerding
Text © 1994, WLP

Chant, Mode IV

Prayer

The ministers and assembly continue to watch and pray.

GOOD FRIDAY

GOOD FRIDAY

PRAYER DURING THE MORNING WATCH

Hymn

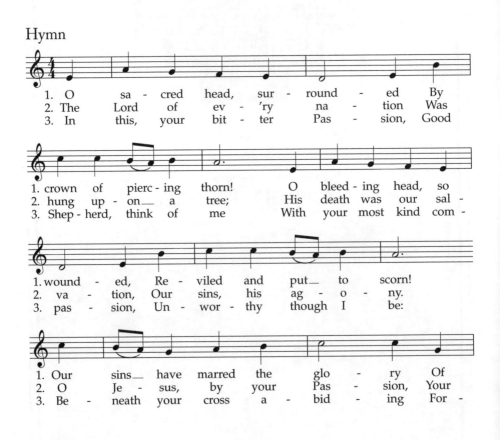

1. O sa - cred head, sur - round - ed By
2. The Lord of ev - 'ry na - tion Was
3. In this, your bit - ter Pas - sion, Good

1. crown of pierc - ing thorn! O bleed - ing head, so
2. hung up - on a tree; His death was our sal -
3. Shep - herd, think of me With your most kind com -

1. wound - ed, Re - viled and put to scorn!
2. va - tion, Our sins, his ag - o - ny.
3. pas - sion, Un - wor - thy though I be:

1. Our sins have marred the glo - ry Of
2. O Je - sus, by your Pas - sion, Your
3. Be - neath your cross a - bid - ing For -

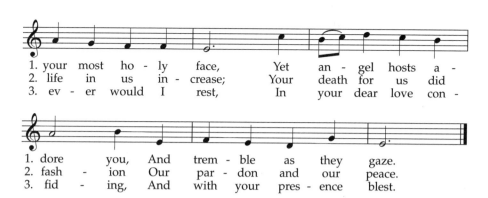

1. your most ho - ly face, Yet an - gel hosts a -
2. life in us in - crease; Your death for us did
3. ev - er would I rest, In your dear love con -

1. dore you, And trem - ble as they gaze.
2. fash - ion Our par - don and our peace.
3. fid - ing, And with your pres - ence blest.

Salve caput cruentatum
Attr. to Bernard of Clairvaux, c. 1091–1153
Vs. 1: Tr. by Henry W. Baker, 1821–1877, alt.
Vs. 2: Melvin L. Farrell, 1930–1986, alt.
Vs. 3: Arthur T. Russell, 1806–1874, alt.
Text (vs. 2) © 1961, WLP

Hans L. Hassler, 1564–1612

Psalmody

Psalm 51

Be mer - ci - ful, O Lord, for we have sinned.

Text © 1969, ICEL

Michael Ward
Music © 1987, WLP

Psalm Prayer

Psalm 22

My God, my God, why have you a - ban - doned me?—

Music © 1995, WLP

Richard T. Proulx

Psalm Prayer

Reading

Isaiah 51:13–15

Canticle of Zechariah

1. Blest be the God of Is - ra - el Who sets all peo - ple
2. God's prom - ised mer - cy will be shown And cov - e - nant re -
3. My child, as proph - et of the Lord, You will pre - pare his

1. free And rais - es up new hope for us: A
2. called, The oath once sworn to A - bra - ham: From
3. way, To tell his peo - ple they are saved From

1. Branch from Da - vid's tree. So have the proph - ets
2. foes to free us all, That we might serve God
3. sin's e - ter - nal sway. Then shall God's mer - cy

1. long de - clared That with a might - y arm God
2. with - out fear And ev - er sing God's praise In
3. from on high Shine forth and nev - er cease To

1. would turn back our en - e - mies And all who wish us harm.
2. ho - li - ness and right - eous - ness Be - fore God all our days.
3. drive a - way the gloom of death And lead us in - to peace.

Carl P. Daw, Jr.
Text © 1989, Hope Publishing Co.

Steven R. Janco
Music © 1994, WLP

Intercessory Prayer

Cantor/Choir   *All*

...let us pray to the Lord. Lord, hear our prayer.
or Lord, have mer - cy.

Byzantine chant

Lord's Prayer

Closing Prayer

The ministers and assembly continue to watch and pray.

GOOD FRIDAY

CELEBRATION OF THE LORD'S PASSION

The Sacred Triduum continues as God gathers us once again before the cross. In simple fashion, we kneel or lie prostrate in an act of humble reverence at the power of this sacred moment. We hear about God's suffering servant and Jesus, our great high priest. These Scriptures open us to the proclamation of the Passion of our Lord Jesus Christ as recorded by John. In John's account, Jesus' final hours are all about the accomplishment of his mission. At the moment of recognition that this man is indeed Jesus the Nazorene, the very ones who come to arrest him fall to the ground. Jesus is the true victor in his arguments with Pilate. Finally, Jesus takes and carries the cross by himself. In the final moment of his life, Jesus utters, "It is finished." What he came to this world to do—to save us from sin and open the way to everlasting life with God—has been accomplished in this most horrible act of violence against the Just One, the Anointed One of God.

After recalling Christ's triumphant death, we remember those who are in need of God's presence and power. We pray today for the Church and its leaders, for those preparing for baptism, for Christian unity, for the Jewish people, for those who do not believe in God or in Christ, for those in public office, and for all in special need.

In a holy moment of grace, we are called to venerate the wood of the cross. When we come before this sign of both struggle and victory, we remember those who are still unjustly condemned; those who suffer in body, mind, and spirit; those who are still being crucified with Christ; and those who have known the victory of the cross. We remember the crosses we are asked to bear. We join all these crosses to the wood of the cross, on which hung the Savior of the world. As believers, we know that the story does not end with the cross. The resurrection is the definitive answer to the horror of Christ's death.

Finally, we are called to come forward to receive the Body of Christ. We know that whenever we eat this bread, we proclaim his death until he comes again. Once again, our celebration of the Sacred Triduum leaves us open to the grace of God at work in these rites. With the Church throughout the world, we await the light of Christ, the light that will dispel the darkness of our hearts.

Part One: Liturgy of the Word

First Reading   *Isaiah 52:13—53:12*

Responsorial Psalm   *Psalm 31:2, 6, 12–13, 15–17, 25*

R/. Fa - ther,——— in - to your hands I com - mend my spir - it.

Music © 1999, WLP   Howard Hughes

Second Reading   *Hebrews 4:4–16; 5:7–9*

Gospel Acclamation

R/. Praise and hon - or to you, Lord Je - sus Christ! Christ!

Music © 1994, WLP   Paul M. French

Gospel   *John 18:1—19:42*

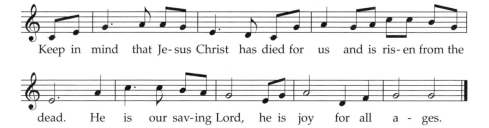

Keep in mind that Je-sus Christ has died for us and is ris-en from the
dead. He is our sav-ing Lord, he is joy for all a - ges.

2 Tm 2:8–12

Lucien Deiss
Text and music © 1965, WLP

Homily

General Intercessions

Let us kneel.

Let us stand.

Part Two: Veneration of the Cross

Showing the Cross

This is the wood of the cross, on which hung the Sav-ior of the world.

R/. Come, let us wor - ship.

Veneration of the Cross

Crux fi - de - lis; cross of glad - ness,
tree on which our hope is___ hung;
Let my arms be as your branch - es!
Yours, the song___ that___ must be___ sung.

Steven C. Warner
Text and music © 1996, WLP

— or —

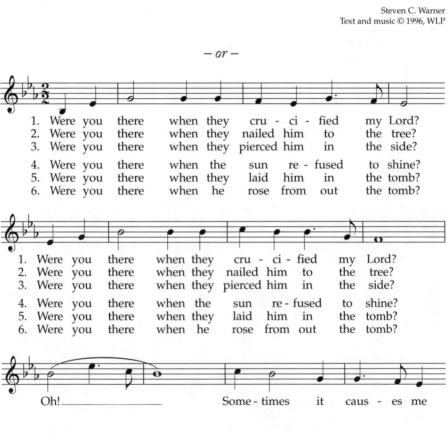

1. Were you there when they cru - ci - fied my Lord?
2. Were you there when they nailed him to the tree?
3. Were you there when they pierced him in the side?
4. Were you there when the sun re - fused to shine?
5. Were you there when they laid him in the tomb?
6. Were you there when he rose from out the tomb?

1. Were you there when they cru - ci - fied my Lord?
2. Were you there when they nailed him to the tree?
3. Were you there when they pierced him in the side?
4. Were you there when the sun re - fused to shine?
5. Were you there when they laid him in the tomb?
6. Were you there when he rose from out the tomb?

Oh!___ Some - times it caus - es me

to trem - ble, trem - ble, trem - ble!

1. Were you there when they cru - ci - fied my Lord?
2. Were you there when they nailed him to the tree?
3. Were you there when they pierced him in the side?
4. Were you there when the sun re - fused to shine?
5. Were you there when they laid him in the tomb?
6. Were you there when he rose from out the tomb?

Traditional African-American Spiritual

Part Three: Holy Communion

Lord's Prayer

Communion Procession

We hold the death of the Lord deep in our hearts._____

Liv-ing, now we re - main with Je- sus, the Christ._____

2 Cor; 1 Jn; 2 Tm

David Haas
Text and music © 1983, GIA

The ministers and members of the assembly depart in solemn silence,
so those remaining to watch and pray may observe holy silence.

HOLY SATURDAY

HOLY SATURDAY

PRAYER DURING THE MORNING WATCH

Hymn

1. What won-drous love is this, O my soul, O my soul!
2. To God and to the Lamb, I will sing, I will sing;
3. And when from death I'm free, I'll sing on, I'll sing on;

1. What won-drous love is this, O my soul!_____
2. To God and to the Lamb I will sing;_____
3. And when from death I'm free, I'll sing on;_____

1. What won-drous love is this, That caused the Lord of bliss
2. To God and to the Lamb Who is the great "I Am,"
3. And when from death I'm free, I'll sing and joy-ful be,

1. To bear the dread-ful curse for my soul, for my soul,
2. While mil-lions join the theme, I will sing, I will sing;
3. And through e-ter-ni-ty I'll sing on, I'll sing on;

1. To bear the dread-ful curse for my soul! _____
2. While mil-lions join the theme, I will sing. _____
3. And through e-ter-ni-ty I'll sing on. _____

Alexander Means, 1801–1883

William Walker's *Southern Harmony*, 1835

Psalmody

Psalm 17

Lord, bend your ear and hear my prayer.

Text (ref.) © 1969, ICEL

Jeffrey Honoré
Text (vss.) and music © 1994, WLP

Psalm Prayer

Psalm 116

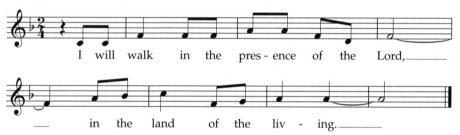

I will walk in the pres-ence of the Lord, _____

_____ in the land of the liv-ing. _____

Text © 1969, ICEL

Howard L. Hughes
Music © 1994, WLP

Psalm Prayer

Reading

Hosea 5:15—16:2

Canticle of Zechariah

1. Blest be the God of Is - ra - el Who sets all peo - ple
2. God's prom - ised mer - cy will be— shown And cov - e - nant re -
3. My child, as proph- et of the— Lord, You will pre - pare his

1. free And rais - es up new hope for— us: A
2. called, The— oath once sworn to A - bra - ham: From
3. way, To— tell his peo - ple they are— saved From

1. Branch from Da - vid's tree. So have the proph - ets
2. foes to free us all, That we might serve God
3. sin's e - ter - nal sway. Then shall God's mer - cy

1. long de - clared That with a might - y arm God
2. with - out fear And ev - er sing God's praise In—
3. from on high Shine forth and nev - er cease To—

1. would turn back our en - e - mies And all who wish us harm.
2. ho - li - ness and right- eous- ness Be - fore God all our days.
3. drive a - way the gloom of— death And lead us in - to peace.

Carl P. Daw, Jr.
Text © 1989, Hope Publishing Co.

Steven R. Janco
Music © 1994, WLP

Intercessory Prayer

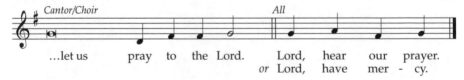

Cantor/Choir   *All*

...let us pray to the Lord. Lord, hear our prayer.
or Lord, have mer - cy.

Byzantine chant

Lord's Prayer

Closing Prayer

The ministers and assembly continue to watch and pray

*H*OLY *S*ATURDAY

PREPARATION RITES FOR THE ELECT

When these rites are celebrated as part of Prayer During the Morning Watch,
they begin following the Canticle of Zechariah.

When these rites are celebrated outside of Prayer During the Morning Watch,
the following refrain may be sung:

Hymn

Blest are we who hear the word of God, Who hear the word of God and keep it. Let us then re-ceive what we now hear, Be-lieve what we re-ceive, And be-come what we be-lieve.

Vince Ambrosetti
Text and music © 1992, 1993, International Liturgy Publications

Greeting

Reading
Mark 7:31–37
Ephphetha, that is, be opened.

– or –

Matthew 16:13–17
You are Christ, the Son of the living God.

– or –

John 6:35, 63–71
To whom shall we go? You have the words of eternal life.

Homily

Ephphetha Rite

"Ephphetha: that is, be opened,
that you may profess the faith you hear,
to the praise and glory of God."

Recitation of the Creed

Prayer

*The Elect recite the Nicene Creed, the profession of faith
in which they will be baptized this night.*

We believe in one God,
the Father, the Almighty,
maker of heaven and earth,
of all that is seen and unseen.

We believe in one Lord, Jesus Christ,
the only Son of God,
eternally begotten of the Father,
God from God, Light from Light,
true God from true God,
begotten, not made, one in Being
    with the Father.
Through him all things were made.

For us men and for our salvation
he came down from heaven:
by the power of the Holy Spirit
he was born of the Virgin Mary,
    and became man.
For our sake he was crucified
    under Pontius Pilate;
he suffered, died, and was buried.

On the third day he rose again
in fulfillment of the Scriptures;
he ascended into heaven
and is seated at the right hand
    of the Father.
He will come again in glory
    to judge the living and the dead,
and his kingdom will have no end.

We believe in the Holy Spirit, the Lord,
    the giver of life,
who proceeds from the Father
    and the Son.
With the Father and the Son
    he is worshiped and glorified.
He has spoken through the Prophets.
We believe in one holy catholic
    and apostolic Church.
We acknowledge one baptism for the
    forgiveness of sins.
We look for the resurrection of the dead,
and the life of the world to come. Amen.

Prayer of Blessing

The assembly may extend their hands in blessing over the Elect.

*When these rites are celebrated as part of Prayer During the Morning Watch,
resume with Intercessory Prayer.*

*When these rites are celebrated outside of Prayer During the Morning Watch,
conclude with the dismissal.*

Dismissal

$\mathcal{H}$OLY $\mathcal{S}$ATURDAY

THE EASTER VIGIL

This is the night when Christians everywhere celebrate the passage of Jesus Christ from death to life. As the Sacred Triduum continues, we first gather in the darkness to kindle a new fire, in anticipation that we will be inflamed with new hope. Christ our Light is proclaimed, and as the Easter light spreads throughout the assembly, we marvel at the power of the Resurrection of Christ.

This is the night when we attune our ears to the power of God's word. Like those who sit around campfires and tell stories, we gather around the flame of the Easter candle and share the greatest stories of our Judeo-Christian treasury. We hear the central stories of salvation that lead us to embrace the story of Christ's triumph over death. "He is not here, he is risen!"

This is the night when those who have traveled the long road of initiation open themselves to the abundant grace poured out in the sacraments. How fitting that this journey of three sacred days brings us to celebrate the sacraments of Baptism, Confirmation, and Eucharist. With fulsome energy and bold symbols, the Church plunges these new ones into the saving waters of Baptism, anoints them with the fragrant Oil of Chrism, and shares, in the most celebratory way we know how, the very body and blood of Christ himself. As the neophytes "put on Christ," this place echoes with our Alleluias. We ring out our joy at Christ's risen presence within these newly baptized and within us.

This is the night when we who have traveled the Lenten journey once again remember the moment when we were baptized into Christ. We hold lighted candles and renounce Satan, the prince of darkness. We boldly make our profession of faith and encounter the waters of Baptism. Through these words and gestures, we are reminded that in our own Baptism, we "put on Christ" and were made into disciples for the life of the world.

This is the night when, having shared in the paschal mystery once again, we renew our commitment to go forth in peace to love and serve the Lord. With Alleluias on our lips, with the fragrance of chrism filling our heads, with fresh baptismal waters covering us, with the taste of bread and wine on our tongues, we go forth renewed in spirit to bring the message of a risen Savior to a world hungry for salvation. This is the night. Alleluia! Alleluia!

HOLY SATURDAY

THE EASTER VIGIL
NIGHTWATCH OF
THE LORD'S RESURRECTION

Part One: The Service of Light

Greeting

Blessing of the New Fire

Preparation of the Paschal Candle

Deacon/Celebrant Christ— our— light.—— *All* Thanks— be to God.——

Procession

Easter Proclamation: The Exsultet

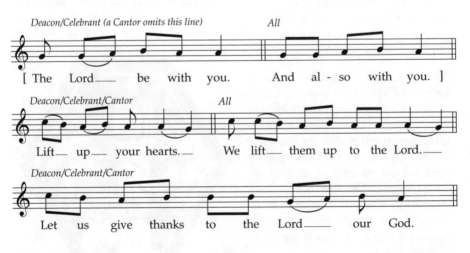

Deacon/Celebrant (a Cantor omits this line) [The Lord— be with you. *All* And al - so with you.]

Deacon/Celebrant/Cantor Lift— up— your hearts.— *All* We lift— them up to the Lord.—

Deacon/Celebrant/Cantor Let us give thanks to the Lord— our God.

It is right to give him thanks—— and praise.——

It is truly right...for ever and ever.

A - men.——

Sacramentary, 1974

Part Two: Liturgy of the Word

First Reading

Genesis 1:1—2:2
or Genesis 1:1, 26–31a

Responsorial Psalm

Psalm 104:1–2, 5–6, 10, 12, 13–14, 24, 35

R/. Lord, send out your Spir-it, and re-new the face of the earth.

Carl F. Schalk

— *or* —

Psalm 33:4–5, 6–7, 12–13, 20–22

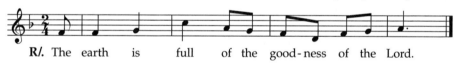

R/. The earth is full of the good-ness of the Lord.

Howard L. Hughes

Second Reading

Genesis 22:1–18
or Genesis 22:1–2, 9a, 10–13, 15–18

Responsorial Psalm

Psalm 16:5, 8, 9–10, 11

R/. You are my in - her-it-ance, O Lord!

You are my in - her-it-ance, O Lord!

Paul A. Lisicky

Third Reading
Exodus 14:15—15:1

Responsorial Psalm
Exodus 15:1–2, 3–4, 5–6, 17–18

R/. I will sing to the Lord whose glo-ry is tri-um-phant;

horse and rid-er have been cast in-to the sea.

To Verses

Final

Horse and rid-er have been cast in-to the sea.

Gael Berberick
Text and music © 1997, WLP

Fourth Reading
Isaiah 54:5–14

Responsorial Psalm
Psalm 30: 2, 4, 5–6, 11–12, 13

R/. I will praise you, Lord, I will praise you,

Lord, for you have res-cued me.

Music © 2000, WLP

Steven C. Warner

Fifth Reading
Isaiah 55:1–11

Responsorial Psalm
Isaiah 12:2–3, 4, 5–6

R/. You will draw wa-ter joy-ful-ly from the

springs of sal-va-tion.

Music © 1984, WLP

Donald J. Reagan

Sixth Reading

Baruch 3:9–15, 32—4:4

Responsorial Psalm

Psalm 19: 8, 9, 10, 11

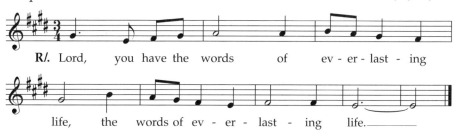

R/. Lord, you have the words of ev-er-last-ing life, the words of ev-er-last-ing life.

Music © 1987, WLP

Marty Haugen

Seventh Reading

Ezekiel 36:16–17a, 18–28

Responsorial Psalm

When baptism is celebrated: *Psalm 42: 3, 5; 43:3, 4*

R/. Like a deer that longs for run-ning streams, my soul longs for you, my God.

Music © 1999, WLP

Richard T. Proulx

When baptism is not celebrated: *Psalm 51: 12–13, 14–15, 18–19*

R/. Cre-ate a clean heart in me, O God.

Music © 1999, WLP

Rory Cooney

Or, when baptism is not celebrated:

The response following the fifth reading,
on page 38, may be sung.

Gloria

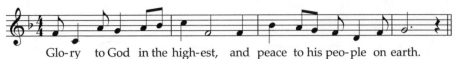

Glo-ry to God in the high-est, and peace to his peo-ple on earth.

Cantor/Choir: Lord God, heavenly King, almighty God and Father,
we worship you,

Glo - ry to God.

Cantor/Choir: We give you thanks,

Glo - ry to God.

Cantor/Choir: We praise you for your glory. *(To Refrain)*

Cantor/Choir: Lord Jesus Christ, only Son of the Father,
Lord, God, Lamb of God, you take away the sin of the world:
have mercy on us,

have mer - cy on us;

Cantor/Choir: You are seated at the right hand of the Father: receive our prayer,

re - ceive— our prayer.

Cantor/Choir: For you alone are the Holy One, you alone are the Lord;
you alone are the Most High, Jesus Christ,
with the Holy Spirit in the glory of God the Father. *(To Refrain)*

A - men! A - men!

Steven R. Janco
Music © 1992, WLP

Opening Prayer

Epistle   *Romans 6:3–11*

Responsorial Psalm - The Easter Alleluia   *Psalm 118: 1–2, 16–17, 22–23*

R/. Al - le - lu - ia,___ al - le - lu - ia, al - le - lu - ia.

Mode II

Gospel   *Year A: Matthew 28:1–10*
                                                     Year B: Mark 16:1–7
                                                     Year C: Luke 24:1–12

Homily

Part Three: Celebration of the Sacraments of Initiation and the Rite of Reception into the Full Communion of the Catholic Church

Celebration of Baptism

Presentation of the Candidates for Baptism

Invitation to Prayer

Litany of the Saints

Cantor   *All*   *Cantor*
Lord, have mer - cy. Lord, have mer - cy. Christ, have mer - cy.

All   *Cantor*   *All*
Christ, have mer - cy. Lord, have_ mer - cy. Lord, have_ mer - cy.

Holy Mary, Mother of	God,	pray for us.
Saint	Mi - chael,	pray for us.
Holy angels of	God,	pray for us.
Saint John the	Bap - tist,	pray for us.
Saint	Jo - seph,	pray for us.
Saint Peter and Saint	Paul,	pray for
Saint	An - drew,	pray for us.
Saint	John,	pray for us.
Saint Mary	Mag - dalene,	pray for us.
Saint	Ste - phen,	pray for us.
Saint Ig -	na - tius,	pray for us.
Saint	Law - rence,	pray for us.
Saint Perpetua and Saint Fe - lic - ity,		pray for us.
Saint	Ag - nes,	pray for us.
Saint	Gre - gory,	pray for us.
Saint Au -	gus - tine,	pray for us.
Saint Atha -	na - sius,	pray for us.
Saint	Ba - sil,	pray for us.
Saint	Mar - tin,	pray for us.
Saint	Ben - edict,	pray for us.
Saint Francis and Saint	Dom - inic,	pray for us.
Saint Francis	Xa - vier,	pray for us.
Saint John Vi -	an - ney,	pray for us.
Saint	Cath - erine,	pray for us.
Saint Te -	re - sa,	pray for us.
All holy men and	wom - en,	pray for us.

If not already included, patron saints of the church, the place, and the candidates for baptism may be included in the litany.

Cantor   All

Lord, be mer - ci - ful,	Lord, save your	peo - ple.
From all e - vil,	Lord, save your	peo - ple.
From ev - 'ry sin,	Lord, save your	peo - ple.
From ev - er - last - ing death,	Lord, save your	peo - ple.

Cantor   All

By your com - ing as man,	Lord, save your	peo - ple.
By your death and ris - ing to new life,	Lord, save your	peo - ple.
By your gift of the Ho - ly Spir - it,	Lord, save your	peo - ple.

Be merciful to us sin - ners. Lord, hear our prayer.

Other suitable petitions may be added here. If there are candidates for baptism:

Give new life to these chosen ones by the grace of baptism. Lord, hear our prayer.

If there are no candidates for baptism:

By your grace bless this font where your children will be re - born. Lord, hear our prayer.

Jesus, Son of the liv-ing God. Lord, hear our prayer.

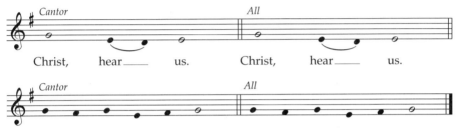

Christ, hear us. Christ, hear us.

Lord Je - sus, hear our prayer. Lord Je - sus, hear our prayer.

Text © 1970, ICEL

Chant

Blessing of the Water

1. Springs of wa - ter, bless the Lord,
2. In - to the wa - ter, bur - ied in death,

Repeat as necessary

1. sing the glo - ry due God's name.
2. we are ris - en to new life.

Mike Hay

Text (vs. 1) © 1973, ICEL

Text (vs. 2) and music © 1994, WLP

Profession of Faith

Renunciation of Sin

Profession of Faith

Baptism

Re - joice, re - joice, child of God! You are bap-tized in Je - sus Christ!

Re - joice, re - joice! Al - le - lu - ia! Al - le-lu - ia!

Lisa L. Stafford
Text and music © 1999, WLP

Explanatory Rites

[Anointing after Baptism]

If confirmation is delayed, the newly baptized are anointed with chrism.

Clothing with a Baptismal Garment

Presentation of a Lighted Candle

Renewal of Baptismal Promises

*The candidates for full communion join the rest of the baptized assembly
in this renunciation of sin and profession of faith.
All stand and hold lighted candles.*

Sprinkling with Baptismal Water

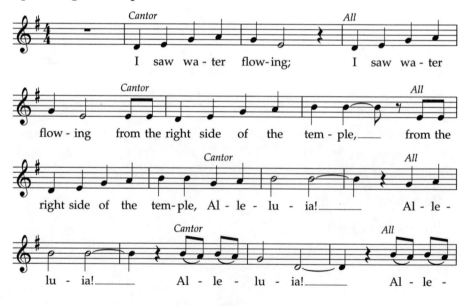

Cantor I saw wa - ter flow-ing; *All* I saw wa - ter

flow - ing from the right side of the tem - ple,___ from the

right side of the tem-ple, Al - le - lu - ia!___ Al - le -

lu - ia!___ Al - le - lu - ia!___ Al - le -

lu - ia!___ The wa - ter brought God's life, the wa - ter brought God's life and God's sal - va - tion, and God's sal - va - tion, and the peo - ple sang in praise; and the peo - ple sang in praise: Al - le - lu - ia! Al - le - lu - ia!___ Al - le - lu - ia!___ Al - le - lu - ia! Al - le - lu - ia!___ Al - le - lu - ia! Al - le - lu - ia!___ Al - le - lu - ia!___

Ez 47:1, 9
The Roman Missal
Text © 1973, ICEL

Michael Ward
Music © 1991, WLP

Celebration of Reception into Full Communion

Invitation

Profession by the Candidates

Act of Reception

Celebration of Confirmation

Invitation

Laying on of Hands

Anointing with Chrism

Come, O Spir - it, come. Come, O Spir - it, come.
Ve - ni, Spi - ri - tus. Ve - ni, Spi - ri - tus.
Ven, Es - pí - ri - tu. Ven, Es - pí - ri - tu.

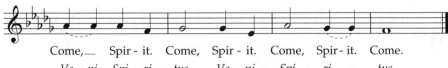

Come,__ Spir - it. Come, Spir - it. Come, Spir - it. Come.
Ve - ni, Spi - ri - tus. Ve - ni, Spi - ri - tus.
Ven, Es - pí - ri - tu. Ven, Es - pí - ri - tu.

Paul F. Page
Text and music © 1994, WLP

General Intercessions

Lord, hear our prayer; De - us, ex - au - di

nos; Se - ñor, es - cú - cha - nos.

Mike Hay (1953–1999)
Music © 1994, WLP

Part Four: Liturgy of the Eucharist

Preparation of the Gifts

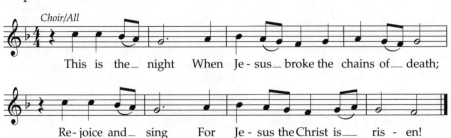

Choir/All
This is the__ night When Je - sus__ broke the chains of__ death;

Re - joice and__ sing For Je - sus the Christ is__ ris - en!

VERSES

Choir

1. This is the night When first you saved our an - ces - tors;
2. This is the night When Chris-tians all are cleansed of___ sin,
3. To-night our hearts, Our homes, our lives are blessed by___ Christ
4. This is the night When Je - sus ran-somed us with his blood

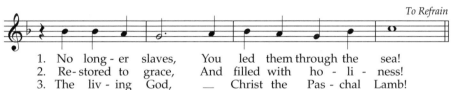

To Refrain

1. No long - er slaves, You led them through the sea!
2. Re - stored to grace, And filled with ho - li - ness!
3. The liv - ing God, ___ Christ the Pas - chal Lamb!
4. And paid for us The price of A - dam's sin!

Adapt. from the *Exsultet*

Jeffrey Schneider
Text and music © 1994, WLP

Eucharistic Prayer

Preface Acclamation

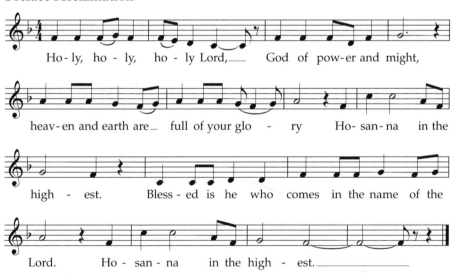

Ho-ly, ho - ly, ho - ly Lord,___ God of pow-er and might,

heav-en and earth are___ full of your glo - ry Ho-san-na in the

high - est. Bless - ed is he who comes in the name of the

Lord. Ho - san - na in the high - est.___

People's Mass
Jan M. Vermulst, 1925–1994
Music © 1970, 1984, WLP

Memorial Acclamation

Christ has died, Christ is ris - en, Christ will come a - gain.

Great Amen

A - men. A - men. A - men.

Danish Amen Mass
David Kraehenbuehl, 1923–1997
Music © 1970, 1973, WLP

Text (Mem. Accl.) © 1973, ICEL

Communion Rite

Lord's Prayer

Sign of Peace

Lamb of God

Lamb of God, you take a - way the sins of the world,

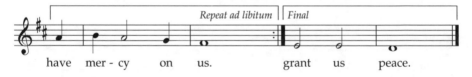

have mer - cy on us. grant us peace.

Holy Cross Mass
David C. Isele
Music © 1979, GIA

Communion Procession

I re- ceived the liv-ing God, and my heart is full of joy.

I re- ceived the liv-ing God, and my heart is full of joy.

Prayer after Communion

Blessing

Easter Dismissal

Thanks be to God, al - le - lu - ia, al - le - lu - ia.___

Hymn

1. Je - sus Christ is ris'n to - day,___
2. Hymns of praise then let us sing,___
3. But the pains which he en - dured,
4. Sing we to our God a - bove,

Al - le - lu - ia!

1. Our tri - um - phant, ho - ly day,___
2. Un - to Christ, our heav'n - ly King,
3. Our sal - va - tion have pro - cured;
4. Praise e - ter - nal, as God's love;___

Al - le - lu - ia!

1. Who did once up - on the cross,
2. Who en - dured the cross and grave,
3. Now he rules, e - ter - nal King,
4. Sing in praise, you heav'n - ly host,

Al - le - lu - ia!

1. Suf - fer___ to re - deem our loss.
2. Sin - ners to re - deem and save.
3. Where the___ an - gels ev - er sing.
4. Fa - ther, Son, and Ho - ly Ghost.

Al - le - lu - ia!

Surrexit Christus hodie
Latin carol, 14th cent.
English text, comp., 18th cent., alt.

Lyra Davidica, 1708
The Compleat Psalmodist, 1749

EASTER SUNDAY

EASTER SUNDAY
THE RESURRECTION OF THE LORD

THE MASS OF EASTER DAY

Hymn

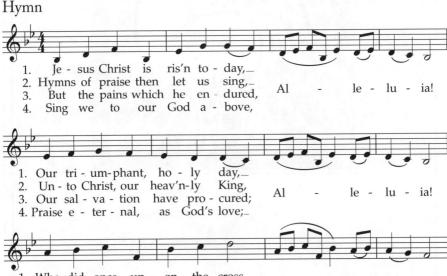

1. Je - sus Christ is ris'n to - day,—
2. Hymns of praise then let us sing,—
3. But the pains which he en - dured,
4. Sing we to our God a - bove,

Al - le - lu - ia!

1. Our tri - um-phant, ho - ly day,—
2. Un - to Christ, our heav'n-ly King,
3. Our sal - va - tion have pro - cured;
4. Praise e - ter - nal, as God's love;—

Al - le - lu - ia!

1. Who did once up - on the cross,
2. Who en-dured the cross and grave,
3. Now he rules, e - ter - nal King,
4. Sing in praise, you heav'n-ly host,

Al - le - lu - ia!

1. Suf - fer— to re - deem our loss.
2. Sin - ners to re - deem and save.
3. Where the— an - gels ev - er sing.
4. Fa - ther, Son, and Ho - ly Ghost.

Al - le - lu - ia!

Surrexit Christus hodie
Latin carol, 14th cent.
English text, comp., 18th cent., alt.

Lyra Davidica, 1708
The Compleat Psalmodist, 1749

Gloria

Glo-ry to God in the high-est, and peace to his peo-ple on earth.

Cantor/Choir: Lord God, heavenly King, almighty God and Father,
we worship you,

Glo - ry to God.

Cantor/Choir: We give you thanks,

Glo - ry to God.

Cantor/Choir: We praise you for your glory. *(To Refrain)*

Cantor/Choir: Lord Jesus Christ, only Son of the Father,
Lord, God, Lamb of God, you take away the sin of the world:
have mercy on us,

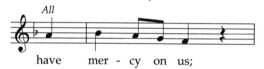

have mer - cy on us;

Cantor/Choir: You are seated at the right hand of the Father: receive our prayer,

re - ceive__ our prayer.

Cantor/Choir: For you alone are the Holy One, you alone are the Lord;
you alone are the Most High, Jesus Christ,
with the Holy Spirit in the glory of God the Father. *(To Refrain)*

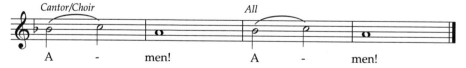

A - men! A - men!

Steven R. Janco
Music © 1992, WLP

Liturgy of the Word

First Reading   *Acts 10:34a, 37–43*

Responsorial Psalm   *Psalm 118:1–2, 16–17, 22–23*

R/. This is the day the Lord____ has made;
let us re-joice and be glad!____   glad!____

Music © 1994, WLP   Alan J. Hommerding

Second Reading   *Colossians 3:1–4*
                                            or 1 Corinthians 5:6b–8

Easter Sequence

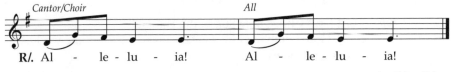

R/. Al - le-lu - ia!   Al - le-lu - ia!

Music © 1996, WLP   Ann Celeen Dohms

Gospel Acclamation

R/. Al - le - lu - ia,____ al - le - lu - ia,   al - le - lu - ia.

Mode II

Gospel   *John 20:1–9*

Homily

Renewal of Baptismal Promises

Sprinkling with Baptismal Water

1. Wa - ters of life, Wa - ters of life,
2. Wa - ters of life, Wa - ters of life,

1. Cre - at - ing life, Cre - at - ing life,
2. Spir - it of God, Spir - it of God,

1. Bap - tized in faith, Bap - tized in faith,
2. Called as your own, Called as your own,

1. Sealed with your love, Sealed with your love.
2. Light for our lives, Light for our lives.

Laura Kutscher
Text and music © 1992, WLP

General Intercessions

Lord, hear our prayer; De - us, ex - au - di nos; Se - ñor, es - cú - cha - nos.

Mike Hay (1953–1999)
Music © 1994, WLP

Liturgy of the Eucharist

Preparation of the Gifts

Hymn

1. Christ is ris - en! Shout Ho - san - na!____ Cel - e -
2. Christ is ris - en! Raise your spir - its____ From the
3. Christ is ris - en! Earth and heav - en____ Nev - er -

1. brate this day of days!____ Christ is ris - en! Hush in
2. cav - erns of de - spair.____ Walk with glad - ness in the
3. more shall be the same.____ Break the bread of new cre -

1. won - der:____ All cre - a - tion is____ a - mazed.__ In the
2. morn - ing.__ See what love can do__ and dare.__ Drink the
3. a - tion__ Where the world is still__ in pain.__ Tell its

1. des - ert all - sur - round - ing,____ See, a spread - ing tree has
2. wine of res - ur - rec - tion,____ Not a serv - ant, but a
3. grim, de - mon - ic chor - us:____ "Christ is ris - en! Get you

1. grown. Heal - ing leaves of grace a - bound - ing____ Bring a
2. friend. Je - sus is our strong com - pan - ion.____ Joy and
3. gone!" God the First and Last is with us.____ Sing Ho -

1. taste of love_ un - known.
2. peace shall nev - er end.
3. san - na ev - 'ry - one!

Brian Wren
Text © 1986, Hope Publishing Co.

Kevin Kelly
Music © 1997, WLP

Eucharistic Prayer

Preface Acclamation

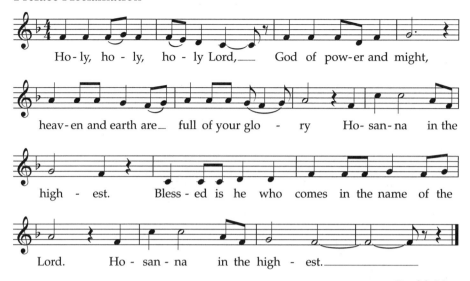

Ho-ly, ho-ly, ho-ly Lord,__ God of pow-er and might,

heav-en and earth are__ full of your glo - ry Ho-san-na in the

high - est. Bless-ed is he who comes in the name of the

Lord. Ho-san-na in the high - est._____

People's Mass
Jan M. Vermulst, 1925–1994
Music © 1970, 1984, WLP

Memorial Acclamation

Christ has died, Christ is ris-en, Christ will come a-gain.

Great Amen

A - men. A - men. A - men.

Danish Amen Mass
David Kraehenbuehl, 1923–1997
Music © 1970, 1973, WLP

Text (Mem. Accl.) © 1973, ICEL

Communion Rite

Lord's Prayer

Sign of Peace

Lamb of God

Lamb_____ of God, you take a-way the sins of the world,

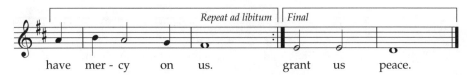

have mer-cy on us. grant us peace.

Holy Cross Mass
David C. Isele
Music © 1979, GIA

Communion Procession

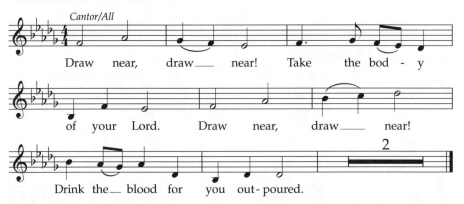

Draw near, draw___ near! Take the bod - y

of your Lord. Draw near, draw___ near!

Drink the__ blood for you out-poured.

Sancti, venite, Christi corpus sumite
7th cent. hymn, tr. by John M. Neale, 1818–1866, alt.

Steven R. Janco
Music © 1992, WLP

Blessing

Easter Dismissal

Thanks be to God, al-le-lu - ia, al-le - lu - ia.___

Closing Hymn

1. Al - le - lu - ia! Al - le - lu - ia! Hearts and voic - es
2. Now the i - ron bars are bro - ken, Christ from death to
3. Christ is ris - en, we are ris - en! Shed up - on us
4. Al - le - lu - ia! Al - le - lu - ia! Glo - ry be to

1. heav'n - ward raise: Sing to God a hymn of glad - ness,
2. life is born, Glo - rious life and life im - mor - tal,
3. heav'n - ly grace, Rain and dew and gleams of glo - ry
4. God on high; Al - le - lu - ia to the Sav - ior

1. Sing to God a hymn of praise. Christ, who on the
2. On that ho - ly Eas - ter morn. Christ has tri - umphed,
3. From your ho - ly ra - diant face; That, with hearts in
4. Who has won the vic - to - ry; Al - le - lu - ia

1. cross a vic - tim, For the world's sal - va - tion bled,
2. and we con - quer By this might - y en - ter - prise,
3. heav - en dwell - ing, We on earth, your ser - vants true,
4. to the Spir - it, Fount of love and sanc - ti - ty;

1. Je - sus Christ, the King of glo - ry,
2. We with Christ to life e - ter - nal
3. Will by an - gel hands be gath - ered,
4. Al - le - lu - ia! Al - le - lu - ia!

1. Now is ris - en from the dead.
2. By his res - ur - rec - tion rise.
3. And be ev - er, Lord, with you.
4. To the Tri - une Maj - es - ty.

Christopher Wordsworth, 1807–1885

Ludwig van Beethoven 1770–1827
Adapt. by Edward Hodges, 1796–1867

59

Easter Sunday Evening

Paschal Vespers

Invitatory

Presider (or Assistant)

Light_____ and peace in Je - sus Christ our Lord.

All

Thanks_____ be to God.

J. Michael Joncas
Music © 1995, WLP

Hymn

1. When dark - ness bids our la - bor cease and
2. For gifts un - earned and yet re - ceived, for
3. This is the day the Lord has made: re -
4. Let ev' - ry voice in har - mo - ny ac -

1. na - ture's eyes have closed in peace, may we, cre - a - tion's
2. things un - seen and yet be - lieved, for trust in your un -
3. joice, no long - er be a - fraid, for, like the am - a -
4. claim the Ho - ly Trin - i - ty. Let earth, in splen - did

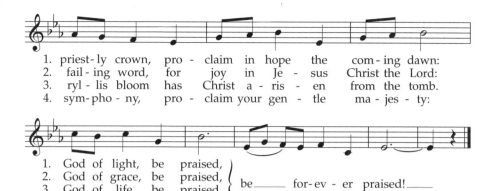

1. priest-ly crown, pro - claim in hope the com-ing dawn:
2. fail-ing word, for joy in Je - sus Christ the Lord:
3. ryl - lis bloom has Christ a - ris - en from the tomb.
4. sym-pho - ny, pro - claim your gen - tle ma - jes - ty:

1. God of light, be praised,
2. God of grace, be praised,
3. God of life, be praised,
4. God of all, be praised,

be_____ for-ev - er praised!_____

Delores Dufner
Text © 1995, Sisters of St. Benedict

J. Michael Joncas
Music © 1995, WLP

Evening Thanksgiving

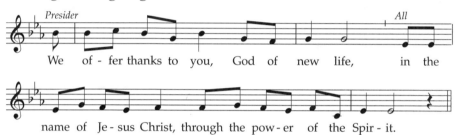

Presider ... *All*

We of - fer thanks to you, God of new life, in the

name of Je - sus Christ, through the pow-er of the Spir - it.

Alan J. Hommerding

J. Michael Joncas
Text and music © 1995, WLP

(last time) Presider/Assistant: "Now and forever, Amen."

All

Now___ and for-ev - er. A - men.

J. Michael Joncas
Music © 1995, WLP

Psalmody

Psalm 136

God's love is ev - er-last - ing; God's love is ev - er-last- ing.___

Music © 1987, WLP

Paul A. Lisicky

Psalm Prayer

Psalm 66

Let all the earth cry out to God with joy, al - le - lu - ia.

Music © 1985, WLP   John H. Olivier

Psalm Prayer

Reading

Hebrews 10:12–14

> *To conclude Paschal Vespers, if convenient, members of the assembly may walk in procession to the Baptismal font as the Canticle of Mary is sung.*

Canticle of Mary

1. Sing, my soul, sing out your prais - es; Sing, for
2. Hearts of pride our God will scat - ter, Haught - y
3. Glo - ry be to God al - might - y, Guid - ing

1. God ex - alt - ed me. Look - ing on this
2. ones will be cast down, Rais - ing those who
3. us in per - fect love. Glo - ry be to

1. low - ly ser - vant, All shall bless me ten - der - ly.
2. once were low - ly, Feed - ing all who are God's own.
3. Je - sus, Sav - ior, God's own Word from heav'n a - bove.

1. Might - y God has shown great fa - vor, Ho - ly
2. Is - ra - el, up - held in mer - cy, Knows the
3. Glo - ry be to God the Spir - it, Might - y

1. is that won - drous name. Mer - ci - ful to
2. heav'n - ly, prom - ised grace Giv'n to A - bra -
3. wind and burn - ing fire. Saints and sin - ners,

1.	all earth's	chil-dren,	Age	to—	age,	God	loves	the	same.
2.	ham and	Sa - rah,	Par - ents	of	our—	cho - sen	race.		
3.	join in	sing - ing	With the	blest,	ce -	les - tial	choir.		

Alan J. Hommerding
Text © 1994, WLP

Joshua Leavitt's *Christian Lyre*, 1830

Intercessory Prayer

All

Hear us as we pray, hear us as we pray, God of life e - ter-nal.

Alan J. Hommerding

J. Michael Joncas
Text and music © 1995, WLP

Lord's Prayer

Closing Prayer

Blessing

Presider ... *All*

(...be up - on— you/us:) now— and for-ev - er. A - men.

All (Last time)

now— and for-ev - er. A - men. Now— and for-ev - er. A - men.

Alan J. Hommerding

J. Michael Joncas
Text and music © 1995, WLP

Dismissal

Thanks be to God, al - le-lu - ia, al - le - lu - ia.___

STATIONS OF THE CROSS

Hymn

The Stations of the Cross   *Alan J. Hommerding*

> **Introductory verse**   (tune: STABAT MATER DOLOROSA)
>
> Jesus kneels, in sorrow praying,
> Knows his fate, God's will obeying:
> "Let your will, not mine, be done."

Greeting

Opening Prayer

I

Presider: **The First Station:**
                    Jesus is sentenced to death.

Kneel

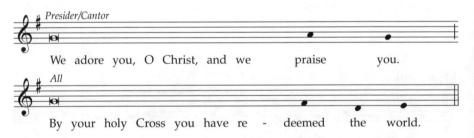

Presider/Cantor

We adore you, O Christ, and we praise you.

All

By your holy Cross you have re - deemed the world.

Stand

Reader: *Luke 38:1–2, 23–24*

All: *Psalm 64:3–4*

    Hide me from the malicious crowd,
      the mob of evildoers.
    They sharpen their tongues like swords,
      ready their bows for arrows of poison words.

The Stations of the Cross ~ Verse 1

Meeting Pilate's earthly power,
Jesus lives these final hours
Confident in heaven's might.

II

Presider: **The Second Station:**

    Jesus accepts the cross.

Kneel

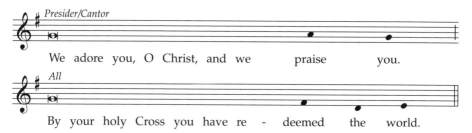

We adore you, O Christ, and we praise you.

By your holy Cross you have re - deemed the world.

Stand

Reader: *Matthew 27:27–31*

All: *Isaiah 53:7*

    Like a lamb led to the slaughter
      or a sheep before the shearers,
      he was silent and opened not his mouth.

The Stations of the Cross ~ Verse 2

In the weight of crossbeams wooden
Jesus feels the heavy burden
Of our frail humanity.

III

Presider:

The Third Station:
Jesus falls the first time.

Kneel

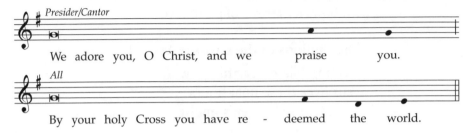

Presider/Cantor
We adore you, O Christ, and we praise you.

All
By your holy Cross you have re - deemed the world.

Stand

Reader: *Isaiah 53:4–6*

All: *Corinthians 5:2*

For in his tent we groan,
longing to be further clothed with our heavenly habitation.

The Stations of the Cross ~ Verse 3

Stumbling under weight so crushing,
Jeering crowds upon him rushing,
Jesus falls, returns to dust.

IV

Presider:

The Fourth Station:
Jesus meets his mother Mary.

Kneel

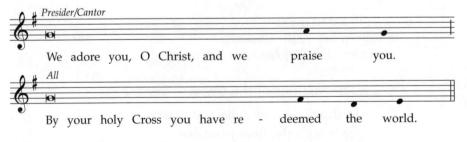

Presider/Cantor
We adore you, O Christ, and we praise you.

All
By your holy Cross you have re - deemed the world.

Stand

Reader: *Isaiah 66:10, 12–13*

All: *John 16:20*

> You will weep and mourn while the world rejoices;
> you will grieve, but your grief will be turned into joy.

The Stations of the Cross ~ Verse 4

> She who knew her heart, in sorrow
> Would be pierced, here bravely follows
> In her Son's distress and pain.

V

Presider: **The Fifth Station:**

Simon helps Jesus carry the cross.

Kneel

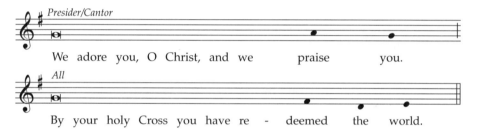

We adore you, O Christ, and we praise you.

By your holy Cross you have re - deemed the world.

Stand

Reader: *Luke 23:26–27*

All: *Matthew 16:24*

> If you wish to come after me,
> deny yourself, take up your cross, and follow me.

The Stations of the Cross ~ Verse 5

> Simon, one with Jesus bearing,
> Shows the way of our own sharing,
> Taking up our daily cross.

<h1 style="text-align:center">VI</h1>

Presider:

<h2 style="text-align:center">The Sixth Station:</h2>
Veronica wipes the face of Jesus.

Kneel

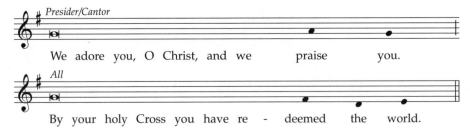

Presider/Cantor

We adore you, O Christ, and we praise you.

All

By your holy Cross you have re - deemed the world.

Stand

Reader: *Sirach 6:14–15*

All: *John 13:34*

> I give you a new commandment: love one another.
> As I have loved you,
> so you should love one another.

<h3 style="text-align:center">The Stations of the Cross ~ Verse 6</h3>

> Boldly facing disapproval
> She, in cleansing, sought removal
> Of the stains of agony.

<h1 style="text-align:center">VII</h1>

Presider:

<h2 style="text-align:center">The Seventh Station:</h2>
Jesus falls a second time.

Kneel

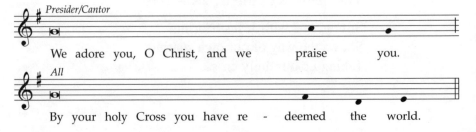

Presider/Cantor

We adore you, O Christ, and we praise you.

All

By your holy Cross you have re - deemed the world.

Stand

Reader: *Song of Songs 5:7–8*

All: *Philippians 2:8*

He humbled himself,
becoming obedient to death,
death on a cross.

The Stations of the Cross ~ Verse 7

Falling once again, Lord Jesus
Shows the suffering that frees us
As we struggle on our way.

VIII

Presider: **The Eighth Station:**

Jesus speaks to the women of Jerusalem.

Kneel

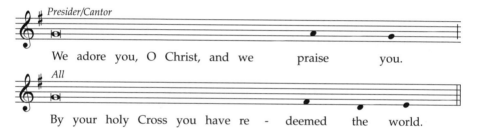

Presider/Cantor

We adore you, O Christ, and we praise you.

All

By your holy Cross you have re - deemed the world.

Stand

Reader: *Luke 23:27–28*

All: *Ruth 1:16*

Ruth said: "Do not ask me to abandon or forsake you!
for wherever you go I will go, wherever you lodge I will lodge;
your people shall be my people, and your God my God."

The Stations of the Cross ~ Verse 8

Israel's own daughters, weeping
Came to Jesus, comfort seeking
In the time of their distress.

IX

Presider:

The Ninth Station:
Jesus falls a third time.

Kneel

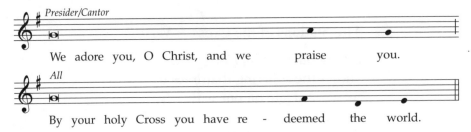

We adore you, O Christ, and we praise you.

By your holy Cross you have re - deemed the world.

Stand

Reader: *John 12:24*

All: *Isaiah 38:12, 14*

> You have folded up my life, like a weaver
> who severs the last thread.
> Like a swallow I utter shrill cries;
> I moan like a dove.

The Stations of the Cross ~ Verse 9

Jesus weakened, bruised and feeble,
Falls again, appears unable
To complete his painful road.

X

Presider:

The Tenth Station:
Jesus is stripped of his garments.

Kneel

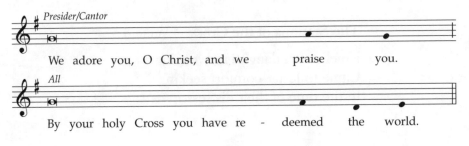

We adore you, O Christ, and we praise you.

By your holy Cross you have re - deemed the world.

Stand

70

Reader: *Mark 15:22–24*

All: *Job 1:21*

Naked I came forth from my mother's womb,
and naked shall I go back again.
The LORD gave and the LORD has taken away;
blessed be the name of the Lord!

The Stations of the Cross ~ Verse 10

Naked, stark, in desolation,
Jesus knows humiliation,
Robbed of his last dignity.

XI

Presider:

The Eleventh Station:
Jesus is crucified.

Kneel

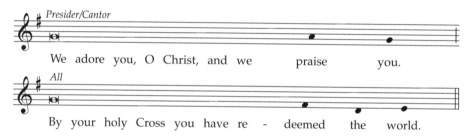

We adore you, O Christ, and we praise you.

By your holy Cross you have re - deemed the world.

Stand

Reader: *Luke 23:33–34*

All: *John 3:14–15*

Just as Moses lifted up the serpent in the desert,
so must the Son of Man be lifted up,
so that everyone who believes in him may have eternal life.

The Stations of the Cross ~ Verse 11

Hands which heal and bless and feed us,
Feet which to the kingdom lead us,
Now are pierced with cruel steel.

XII

Presider:

The Twelfth Station:

Jesus dies on the cross.

Kneel

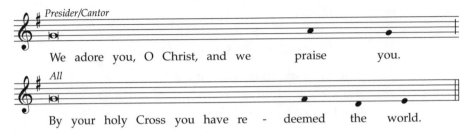

Presider/Cantor

We adore you, O Christ, and we praise you.

All

By your holy Cross you have re - deemed the world.

Stand

Reader: *Mark 15:33–37*

All: *John 16:33*

I have told you this so that you might have peace in me.
In the world you will have trouble, but take courage,
I have conquered the world.

The Stations of the Cross ~ Verse 12

There between the earth and heaven
Death appears, in triumph, proven:
Jesus draws his dying breath.

XIII

Presider: **The Thirteenth Station:**

Jesus' mother and friends lower his body from the cross.

Kneel

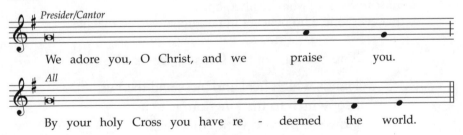

Presider/Cantor

We adore you, O Christ, and we praise you.

All

By your holy Cross you have re - deemed the world.

Stand

Reader: *Luke 23:50–53*

All: *Lamentations 1:12*

> Come, all you who pass by the way,
> look and see
>> Whether there is any suffering like my suffering.

The Stations of the Cross ~ Verse 13

> Oh what sorrow, pain and anguish
> Comes to those who saw him perish
> As they take his body down.

XIV

Presider: **The Fourteenth Station:**

Jesus' mother and friends lay his body in the tomb.

Kneel

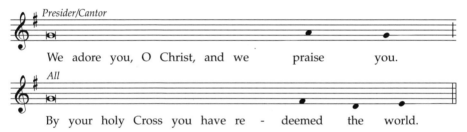

Presider/Cantor

We adore you, O Christ, and we praise you.

All

By your holy Cross you have re - deemed the world.

Stand

Reader: *Matthew 27:59–60*

All: *Psalm 62:6*

> My soul, be at rest in God alone,
>> from whom comes my hope.

The Stations of the Cross ~ Verse 14

> Some believe the awful journey
> Finishes all bleak and stony,
> Yet a new life will arise.

Presider: Let us pray in the words our Savior gave us:

All: Our Father, who art in heaven . . .

Blessing and Dismissal

If Veneration of the Cross is observed, refer to pages 25 through 27.
Following the veneration, the presider prays the closing prayer
and prayer over the people.

Closing Prayer

Prayer Over the People

The Stations of the Cross ~ Concluding verse

Let us walk with Christ while praying
As he did, God's will obeying,
"Let your will, not mine, be done."

TENEBRAE

Tenebrae is the Latin word for "shadows" or "darkness." The Tenebrae service originated in monastic communities. Evening and early morning services for each of the final three days of Holy Week were combined and were anticipated in celebrations during the evenings before each of the great days. The term Tenebrae came into use because candles were extinguished, one by one, as the service progressed. One candle remained at the end of the service and when it was hidden, the community was reminded of Christ's burial. The community then made loud noises until the candle was returned from its hiding place. These loud noises recalled the period of tumult that occurred when Christ died on the cross. The returned candle stood as a sign of the resurrection.

The service presented here is an abbreviated form of Tenebrae. In its purest form, the service can last many hours. The "nocturns" refer to the three services that originally constituted Tenebrae. Seven candles are lighted before the celebration and are extinguished, one by one, as the service unfolds. The making of the noise when the final candle is taken to its place of hiding can be done by rapping on the church pews with a hymnal, book, or the hand.

Procession

> *The ministers enter the church in silence.*

Prayer

THE FIRST NOCTURN

Psalm 69:1–22

> *The antiphon is recited first by the reader, then repeated by the assembly.*
> *The verses of the psalm may be recited antiphonally,*
> *between the left and right sides of the assembly.*

Antiphon:

> Zeal for your house has eaten me up;
> the scorn of those who scorn you has fallen upon me.

L: Save me, God,
> for the waters have reached my neck.

R: I have sunk into the mire of the deep,
> where there is no foothold.
> I have gone down to the watery depths;
> the flood overwhelms me.

L: I am weary with crying out;
   my throat is parched.
   My eyes have failed,
   looking for my God.

R: More numerous than the hairs of my head
   are those who hate me without cause.

   Too many for my strength
   are my treacherous enemies.
   Must I now restore
   what I did not steal?

L: God, you know my folly;
   my faults are not hidden from you.

R: Let those who wait for you, LORD of hosts,
   not be shamed through me.
   Let those who seek you, God of Israel,
   not be disgraced through me.

L: For your sake I bear insult,
   shame covers my face.

R: I have become an outcast to my kin,
   a stranger to my mother's children.

L: Because zeal for your house consumes me,
   I am scorned by those who scorn you.

R: I have wept and fasted,
   but this led only to scorn.

L: I clothed myself in sackcloth;
   I became a byword for them.

R: They who sit at the gate gossip about me;
   drunkards make me the butt of their songs.

L: But I pray to you, LORD,
   for the time of your favor.
   God, in your great kindness answer me
   with your constant help.

R: Rescue me from the mire;
   do not let me sink.
   Rescue me from my enemies
   and from the watery depths.

L: Do not let the floodwaters overwhelm me,
   nor the deep swallow me,
   nor the mouth of the pit close over me.

R: Answer me, Lord, in your generous love;
   in your great mercy turn to me.

L: Do not hide your face from your servant;
   in my distress hasten to answer me!

R: Come and ransom my life;
   because of my enemies redeem me.

L: You know my reproach, my shame, my disgrace;
   before you stand all my foes.

R: Insult has broken my heart, and I am weak;
   I looked for compassion, but there was none,
   for comforters, but found none.

L: Instead they put gall in my food;
   for my thirst they gave me vinegar.

All:
   Zeal for your house has eaten me up;
   the scorn of those who scorn you has fallen upon me.

Reading: The Lamentations of the Prophet Jeremiah

Response:

Je-ru - sa-lem, Je - ru-sa-lem, re - turn to the Lord, your God.

The first candle is extinguished.

THE SECOND NOCTURN

Psalm 22

The refrain of the psalm is first sung by the cantor then repeated by all.

My God,   my   God,   why have you a - ban- doned me?

Music © 1984, WLP   Jerry R. Brubaker

Reading: From the Catecheses of St. John Chrysostom

Response:

Je-ru - sa-lem, Je - ru-sa-lem, re - turn to the Lord, your God.

The second candle is extinguished.

The Third Nocturn

Psalm 88

The antiphon is sung first be the cantor, then repeated by the assembly.
The verses of the psalm are chanted alternately between
the cantor and the assembly.

Antiphon:

I have become like one who hás no strength, lost a - mòng the dead.

Tone 2

Cantor: LORD, my God, I call óut by day;
at night I cry aloud ìn your presence.

All: Let my prayer come befóre you;
incline your ear tò my cry.

C: For my soul is filled with tróubles;
my life draws nèar to Sheol.

A: I am reckoned with those who go down tó the pit;
I am weak, wìthout strength.

C: My couch is amóng the dead,
with the slain who lie ìn the grave.

A: You remember them nó more;
they are cut off fròm your care.

C: You plunged me into the bottom óf the pit,
into the darkness of thè abyss.

A: Your wrath lies heavy upón me;
all your waves crash òver me.

C: Because of you my friends shún me;
you make me lòathsome to them;
Caged in, I cannot éscape;
my eyes grow dìm from trouble.

A: All day I call tó you, LORD;
I stretch out my hànds to you.

C: Do you work wonders fór the Dead?
Do the shades arìse and praise you?

A: Is your love proclaimed ín the grave,
   your fidelity ìn the tomb?

C: Are your marvels declared in the dárkness,
   your righteous deeds in the land òf oblivi͜on?

A: But I cry out tó you, LORD;
   in the morning my prayer còmes before you.

C: Why do you rejéct me, LORD?
   Why hide your fàce from me?

A: I am mortally afflicted sínce my youth;
   lifeless, I suffer your tèrrible blows.

C: Your wrath has swept óver me;
   your terrors have reduced mè to silence.

A: All day they surge round líke a flood;
   from every side they close ìn on me.

C: Because of you companions shún me;
   my only frìend is darkness.

All: *Repeat Antiphon*

Reading: *Hebrews 4:15—5:10; 9:11–15*

Response:

Je-ru - sa-lem, Je - ru-sa-lem,   re -   turn to the Lord, your God.

The third candle is extinguished.

Psalm 63

My soul is thirst-ing for you, O Lord my God.

Music © 1997, WLP   Steven R. Janco

Response:

Je- ru - sa- lem, Je - ru- sa- lem, re - turn to the Lord, your God.

The fourth candle is extinguished.

Canticle of Hezekiah   *Isaiah 38:10–20*

> *The antiphon is recited first by the reader, then repeated
> by the assembly. The canticle is recited, alternating
> between the reader and the assembly.*

Antiphon:
> From the gates of hell, O Lord, deliver my soul.

Reader:
> Once I said,
> > "In the noontime of life I must depart!
> To the gates of the nether world I shall be consigned
> > for the rest of my years."
> I said, "I shall see the LORD no more
> > in the land of the living.

All:
> No longer shall I behold my fellow men
> > among those who dwell in the world."
> My dwelling, like a shepherd's tent,
> > is struck down and borne away from me;
> you have folded up my life,
> > like a weaver who severs the last thread.

Reader:
> Day and night you give me over to torment;
> > I cry out until the dawn.
> Like a lion he breaks all my bones;
> > [day and night you give me over to torment.]

All:

> Like a swallow I utter shrill cries;
>> I moan like a dove.
> My eyes grow weak, gazing heavenward:
>> O LORD, I am in straits; be my surety!

Reader:

> What am I to say or tell him?
>> He has done it!
> I shall go on through all my years
>> despite the bitterness of my soul.
> Those live whom the Lord protects;
>> yours… the life of the spirit.
> You have given me health and life;
>> thus is my bitterness transformed into peace.

All:

> You have preserved my life
>> from the pit of destruction,
> When you cast behind your back
>> all my sins.
> For it is not the nether world that gives you thanks,
>> nor death that praises you;
> Neither do those who go down into the pit
>> await your kindness.

Reader:

> The living, the living give you thanks,
>> as I do today.
> Fathers declare to their sons,
>> O God, your faithfulness.

All:

> The LORD is our savior;
>> we shall sing to stringed instruments
> In the house of the LORD
>> all the days of our life.

All:

> From the gates of hell, O Lord, deliver my soul.

Response:

Je- ru - sa- lem, Je - ru- sa- lem, re - turn to the Lord, your God.

The fifth candle is extinguished.

Psalm 150

The antiphon is sung first by the cantor,
then repeated by the assembly.
The verses of the psalm are chanted alternately
between the cantor and the assembly.

Antiphon:

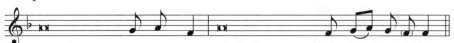

O Death, I will bé your death; O Grave, I will be yòur de - struc - tion.

Tone 6

Cantor: Praise God in his holy sánctuary;
give praise in the mighty dòme of heaven.

All: Give praise for his míghty deeds,
praise him for hìs great majesty.

C: Give praise with blasts upón the horn,
praise him with hàrp and lyre.

A: Give praise with tambourínes and dance,
praise him with flùtes and strings.

C: Give praise with cráshing cymbals,
praise him with sòunding cymbals.

A: Let everything thát has breath
give praise tò the LORD.

All: Antiphon

The sixth candle is extinguished.

All rise.

Canticle of Zechariah

1. Blest be the God of Is - ra - el, The
2. Through ho - ly proph - ets did you speak Your
3. Of old you gave your sol - emn oath To
4. O ti - ny Child, your name shall be The
5. The ris - ing sun shall shine on us To

1. ev - er - liv - ing Lord, You come in pow'r to
2. word in days of old, That you would save us
3. fa - ther A - bra - ham: Whose seed a might - y
4. pro - phet of the Lord; The way of God you
5. bring the light of day To all who dwell in

1. save your own, Your peo - ple Is - ra - el.
2. from our foes And all who bear us ill.
3. race should be And blest for - ev - er - more.
4. shall pre - pare To make God's com - ing known.
5. dark - est night And shad - ow of the grave.

1. For Is - ra - el you now raise up Sal -
2. To our an - ces - tors did you give Your
3. You vowed to set your peo - ple free From
4. You shall pro - claim to Is - ra - el Sal -
5. Our foot - steps God shall safe - ly guide To

1. va - tion's tow'r on high, In Da - vid's house, who
2. cov - e - nant of love; So with us all you
3. fear of ev - 'ry foe, That we might serve you
4. va - tion's dawn - ing day, When God shall wipe a -
5. walk the ways of peace; Whose name for - ev - er -

1. reigned as king And ser - vant of the Lord.
2. keep your word In love that knows no end.
3. all our days In good - ness, love, and peace.
4. way all sins With mer - cy and with love.
5. more be blest, Who lives and loves and saves.

Lk 1:69
James Quinn
Text © James Quinn, Selah Publishing Co. Inc., North American agent

Traditional English folk song
Arr. by Ralph Vaughan Williams, 1872-1958

The final candle is hidden in some nearby place.

All kneel.

The cantor sings the following verse from Philippians.

Christ became obedient to the point of death,
    even death on a cross.
Because of this, God greatly exalted him
    and bestowed on him the name
which is above every other name.

Psalm 51

Re-mem - ber, O Lord,___ your faith-ful-ness___ and love.___

Re-mem - ber, O Lord,___ your faith-ful-ness___ and love.___

Text © 1969, 1981, ICEL

Michael Bedford
Music © 1994, WLP

Prayer

A loud noise is made.
Members of the assembly may join
in the making of this noise.

As the final candle is then brought
from its hiding place, the noise ceases.

By the light of this candle
the ministers and the assembly
depart in silence.

BLESSING OF EASTER FOODS

Hymn

1. At the Lamb's high feast we sing Praise to our vic-
2. Where the pas-chal blood is poured, Death's dark an-gel
3. Might-y Vic-tim from the sky, Hell's fierce pow'rs be-
4. Eas-ter tri-umph, Eas-ter joy, Have the pow'r of

1. to-ri-ous King, Who has washed us in the tide
2. sheathes the sword; Is-rael's hosts tri-um-phant go
3. neath you lie; You have con-quered in the fight,
4. sin de-stroyed. From the pow'r of sin set free,

1. Flow-ing from his wound-ed side; Praise we Christ whose
2. Through the wave that drowns the foe. Praise we Christ whose
3. You have brought us life and light; Now no more can
4. New-born souls in Christ are we. Hymns of glo-ry,

1. love di-vine Gives his sa-cred blood for wine,
2. blood was shed, Pas-chal vic-tim, pas-chal bread;
3. death ap-pall, Now no more the grave en-thrall;
4. songs of praise, Fa-ther, un-to you we raise;

1. Gives his bod-y for the feast, Christ the vic-tim, Christ the priest.
2. With sin-cer-i-ty and love Eat we man-na from a-bove.
3. You have o-pened Par-a-dise, And in you the saints shall rise.
4. Praise to you, our ris-en Lord, And the Spir-it we ac-cord.

Ad regias Agni dapes
Tr. by Robert Campbell, 1814–1868, alt.

Jakob Hintze, 1622–1702

| Minister: | In the name of the Father, and of the Son, and of the Holy Spirit. |
| All: | Amen. |

Before the Easter Vigil

| Minister: | For our sake Christ became obedient, accepting even death, death on a cross. Therefore God raised him on high and gave him the name above all other names. Blessed be God forever. |
| All: | Blessed be God forever. |

Or, after the Easter Vigil

| Minister: | Christ is risen. Alleluia. |
| All: | He is risen indeed. Alleluia. |

| Reading: | *Deuteronomy 16:1–8*
The Passover of the Lord. |

or Isaiah 55:1–11

Come all you who are thirsty.

or Luke 24:13–35

They knew Christ in the breaking of the bread.

or John 6:1–14

Multiplication of the loaves.

Hymn

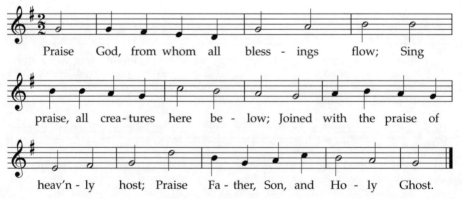

Praise God, from whom all bless - ings flow; Sing praise, all crea-tures here be - low; Joined with the praise of heav'n - ly host; Praise Fa - ther, Son, and Ho - ly Ghost.

Doxology: Thomas Ken, 1637–1711, alt.

Genevan Psalter
Pseaumes octante trois de David, 1551, alt.
Louis Bourgeois, c.1510–c. 1561

Intercessions

Response: "Lord, prepare us for the feast of life."

Lord's Prayer

Prayer of Blessing

Concluding Rite

Hymn

1. For the fruits of all cre - a - tion, Thanks be to God.
2. In the just re - ward of la - bor, God's will is done.
3. For the har - vests of the Spir - it, Thanks be to God.

1. For the gifts to ev - 'ry na - tion, Thanks be to God.
2. In the help we give our neigh-bor, God's will is done.
3. For the good we all in - her - it, Thanks be to God.

1. For the plow - ing, sow - ing, reap - ing, Si - lent
2. In our world - wide task of car - ing For the
3. For the won - ders that as - tound us, For the

1. growth while we are sleep - ing, Fu - ture needs in
2. hun - gry and de - spair - ing, In the har - vests
3. truths that still con - found us, Most of all, that

1. earth's safe-keep - ing, Thanks be to God.
2. we are shar - ing, God's will is done.
3. love has found us, Thanks be to God.

Fred Pratt Green, alt.   Traditional Welsh melody
Text © 1970, Hope Publishing Co.

$\mathcal{A}$DDITIONAL
$\mathcal{M}$USIC

A New Commandment

I___ give you___ a new com- mand - ment:
Love one an - oth - er as___ I have loved___
you, as___ I have loved___ you.

Jn 15:12

Steven R. Janco
Text and music © 1999, WLP

Alleluia! The Strife Is O'er

VICTORY   888 with Alleluias

Al - le - lu - ia! Al - le - lu - ia! Al - le - lu - ia!

1. The strife is o'er, the bat - tle done; Now is the
2. On the third morn he rose___ a - gain, Glo - ri - ous in
3. O ris - en Lord, to you___ we sing. You set us

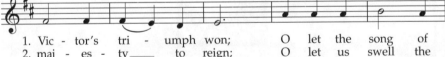

1. Vic - tor's tri - umph won; O let the song of
2. maj - es - ty___ to reign; O let us swell the
3. free from death's cold sting; That all cre - a - tion's

D.C.

1. praise be sung:
2. joy - ful strain: Al - le - lu - ia!
3. song___ may ring:

Symphonia Sirenum Selectarum, Cologne, 1695
Tr. by Francis Pott, 1832–1909, alt.

Giovanni Pierluigi da Palestrina, 1525–1594
Adapt. by William H. Monk, 1823–1889

At the Cross Her Station Keeping

STABAT MATER DOLOROSA 88 7

1. At the cross her sta - tion keep - ing, Stood the mourn - ful
2. Through her heart, his sor - row shar - ing, All his bit - ter
3. Oh, how sad and sore dis - tressed— Was that moth - er

1. moth - er weep - ing, Close to Je - sus to the last.
2. an - guish bear - ing, Now at length the sword has passed.
3. high - ly blest___ Of the sole be - got - ten One!

4. Christ above in torment hangs;
   She beneath beholds the pangs
   Of her dying, glorious Son.

5. Is there one who would not weep,
   'Whelmed in miseries so deep,
   Christ's dear Mother to behold?

6. Can the human heart refrain
   From partaking in her pain,
   In that Mother's pain untold?

7. Bruised, derided, cursed, defiled,
   She beheld her tender Child,
   All with bloody scourges rent.

8. For the sins of his own nation,
   Saw him hang in desolation
   Till his spirit forth he sent.

9. O sweet Mother! fount of love,
   Touch my spirit from above,
   Make my heart with yours accord.

10. Make me feel as you have felt;
    Make my soul to glow and melt
    With the love of Christ, my Lord.

11. Holy Mother, pierce me through,
    In my heart each wound renew
    Of my Savior crucified.

12. Let me share with you his pain,
    Who for all our sins was slain,
    Who for me in torments died.

13. Let me mingle tears with thee,
    Mourning him who mourned for me,
    All the days that I may live:

14. By the cross with you to stay,
    There with you to weep and pray,
    This I ask of you to give.

Ascr. to Jacopone da Todi, c. 1230–1306
Tr. by Edward Caswall, 1814–1878, alt.

(785) *Maintzisch Gesangbuch,* 1661

Baptized in Water

1. Bap-tized in wa - ter, Sealed by the Spir - it, Cleansed by the
2. Bap-tized in wa - ter, Sealed by the Spir - it, Dead in the
3. Bap-tized in wa - ter, Sealed by the Spir - it, Marked with the

1. blood of Christ our King: Heirs of sal - va - tion, Trust-ing his
2. tomb with Christ our King: One with his ris - ing, Freed and for -
3. sign of Christ our King: Born of one Fa - ther, We are his

1. prom - ise, Faith-ful - ly now God's praise we sing.
2. giv - en, Thank-ful - ly now God's praise we sing.
3. chil - dren, Joy - ful - ly now God's praise we sing.

Michael J. Saward
Text © 1982, Hope Publishing Company

(C7) Scots Gaelic melody

Christ the Lord Is Ris'n Today

1. Christ the Lord is ris'n to - day,
2. Lives a - gain our glo - rious King;
3. Love's re - deem - ing work is__ done,
4. Soar we now where Christ has_ led,

Al - le - lu - ia!

1. All on earth with an - gels say.
2. Where, O death, is now your sting?
3. Fought the fight, the bat - tle__ won.
4. Fol - l'wing our ex - alt - ed__ head;

Al - le - lu - ia!

1. Raise your joys and tri - umphs high,
2. Once he died our souls to__ save,
3. Death in vain for - bids him_ rise;
4. Made like him, like him we__ rise,

Al - le - lu - ia!

1. Sing, O heav'ns, and earth re - ply,
2. Where your vic - to - ry, O__ grave?
3. Christ has o - pened par - a - dise.
4. Ours the cross, the grave, the_ skies.

Al - le - lu - ia!

Charles Wesley, 1707–1788

Robert Williams, 1781–1821

Eat This Bread

REFRAIN

Eat this bread, drink this cup, come to me and nev - er be hun - gry.

Eat this bread, drink this cup, trust in me and you will not thirst.

Jn 6:35
Adapt. by Robert J. Batastini and the Taizé Community

Jacques Berthier, 1923–1994
Text and music © 1984, Les Presses de Taizé
Pub. by GIA

Festival Canticle

FESTIVAL CANTICLE   Irregular with Refrain

REFRAIN

This is the feast_____ of vic-to-ry for our God.

Al-le-lu - ia, al-le-lu-ia, al-le-lu - ia!

VERSES

1. Wor - thy is Christ, the_ Lamb who was slain, Whose
2. Pow - er, rich - es,_ wis - dom, and strength, And
3. Sing_____ with all the_ peo - ple of God, And
4. Bless - ing, hon - or,_ glo - ry, and might Be to
5. For_____ the Lamb_____ who was slain Has be -

To Refrain

1. blood set us free_____ to be peo - ple of God.
2. hon - or,_____ bless - ing, and glo - ry are his.
3. join in the hymn of all cre - a - tion.
4. God and the Lamb for - ev - er. A - men.
5. gun his_ reign._ Al - le - lu - ia!

FINAL REFRAIN

This is the feast_____ of vic-to-ry for our God.

Al-le-lu - ia, al-le-lu-ia, al-le-lu - ia!

Adapt. by John W. Arthur, 1922–1980
Text © 1978, Augsburg Fortress

Richard Hillert
Music © 1975, 1988, Richard Hillert

*G*ift of Finest Wheat
BICENTENNIAL   CM with Refrain

You sat-is-fy the hun-gry heart With

gift of fin-est wheat; Come, give to us, O—

sav-ing Lord, The bread of life to eat.——

1. As when the shep-herd calls his sheep, They
2. With joy-ful lips we sing to you Our
3. Is not the cup we bless and share The
4. The mys-t'ry of your pres-ence, Lord, No
5. You give your-self to us, O Lord; Then

1. know and heed his voice, So when you call your
2. praise and grat-i-tude, That you should count us
3. blood of Christ out-poured? Do not one cup, one
4. mor-tal tongue can tell: Whom all the world can -
5. self-less let us be, To serve each oth-er

D.C.

1. fam-'ly, Lord, We fol-low and re-joice.
2. wor-thy, Lord, To share this heav'n-ly food.
3. loaf, de-clare Our one-ness in the Lord?
4. not con-tain Comes in our hearts to dwell.
5. in your name In truth and char-i-ty.

Omer Westendorf, 1916–1997

Robert E. Kreutz, 1922–1996
Text and music © 1977, Archdiocese of Philadelphia

God So Loved the World

Paul A. Tate
Text and music © 1998, WLP

I Know That My Redeemer Lives

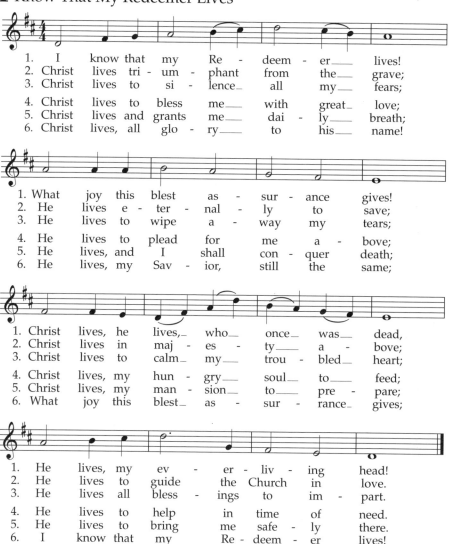

1. I know that my Re - deem - er lives!
2. Christ lives tri - um - phant from the grave;
3. Christ lives to si - lence all my fears;
4. Christ lives to bless me with great love;
5. Christ lives and grants me dai - ly breath;
6. Christ lives, all glo - ry to his name!

1. What joy this blest as - sur - ance gives!
2. He lives e - ter - nal - ly to save;
3. He lives to wipe a - way my tears;
4. He lives to plead for me a - bove;
5. He lives, and I shall con - quer death;
6. He lives, my Sav - ior, still the same;

1. Christ lives, he lives, who once was dead,
2. Christ lives in maj - es - ty a - bove;
3. Christ lives to calm my trou - bled heart;
4. Christ lives, my hun - gry soul to feed;
5. Christ lives, my man - sion to pre - pare;
6. What joy this blest as - sur - ance gives;

1. He lives, my ev - er - liv - ing head!
2. He lives to guide the Church in love.
3. He lives all bless - ings to im - part.
4. He lives to help in time of need.
5. He lives to bring me safe - ly there.
6. I know that my Re - deem - er lives!

Jb 19:25
Samuel Medley, 1738–1799, alt.

Attr. to John Hatton, c. 1710–1793

Jesus Took a Towel

REFRAIN

Je - sus took a tow - el and he gird - ed him - self, Then he

washed my feet, yes, he washed my feet; Je - sus took a ba - sin and he

To Verses

knelt him - self down, And he washed, yes, he washed my feet.

VERSES 1–2

1. The heav - ens are the Lord's, and the earth is his, The
2. The hour had come, the Pasch was near;

1. clouds are his char - iot, glo - ry his cloak; He
2. Je - sus loved his own, loved them to the end. O

1. made the moun - tains, set the lim - its of the sea;
2. Lord, let me see, let me un - der - stand

To Refrain

1. And he stooped and washed my feet.
2. Why you stooped and washed my feet.

VERSES 3–5

3. Je - sus came to Pe - ter; Pe - ter said to him, "Do you
4. Je - sus said to Pe - ter, "Don't you un - der - stand? If you
5. He is King of kings and Lord of lords, Who

3. wash my feet? Lord, do you wash my feet?"
4. want to be mine, I must wash your feet." "Then
5. dwells in light in - ac - ces - si - ble;

3. Je - sus knelt down,_____ but Pe - ter cried
4. not just my feet,___ but my head and my
5. No one has seen him where he sits___ on

3. out, "Lord, you'll nev - er wash my feet!"
4. hands!_____ O Lord, I want to be yours."
5. high, Yet he stooped to wash my feet.

VERSES 6–9

6. "Do you know, lit - tle chil- dren, what I've done for
7. Now friends, let's be glad,— let our joy be
8. Who is like you, Lord,— now en - throned on
9. O the path is rug - ged, and the go - ing is

6. you? You call me Mas- ter, and you call me Lord.
7. full. For God is love, and he a - bides in us.
8. high, Where you look up - on the heav- ens and the earth be- low?
9. rough, The jour - ney is long___ to our heav'n- ly home,

6. If I am your Mas - ter, and if I am your Lord,
7. He washed our feet,_____ he wash - es them still
8. Be - fore your face the earth___ trem - bles and quakes,
9. Our feet are wea - ry___ and cov - ered with mud,

To Refrain

6. Then, what I've done, you must do."
7. When we do what he once did.
8. Yet you stoop to wash my feet!
9. So the Lord still wash - es our feet.

Jn 13

(C55) Chrysogonus Waddell
Text and music © Gethsemani Abbey, used by permission of GIA

Jesus, Remember Me

Je-sus, re-mem-ber me when you come in-to your King-dom.

Je-sus, re-mem-ber me when you come in-to your King-dom.

Jacques Berthier, 1923–1994
Text and music © 1984, Les Presses de Taizé
Pub. by GIA

Let Us Break Bread Together

LET US BREAK BREAD TOGETHER   10 10 with Refrain

1. Let us break bread to-geth-er on our knees;
2. Let us drink wine to-geth-er on our knees;
3. Let us praise God to-geth-er on our knees;

1. Let us break bread to-geth-er on our knees.
2. Let us drink wine to-geth-er on our knees.
3. Let us praise God to-geth-er on our knees.

When I fall on my knees, with my face to the ris-ing

sun, O Lord, have mer-cy on me.

African-American

100

*L*ove Is His Word

DeBLASIO 88 97 with Refrain

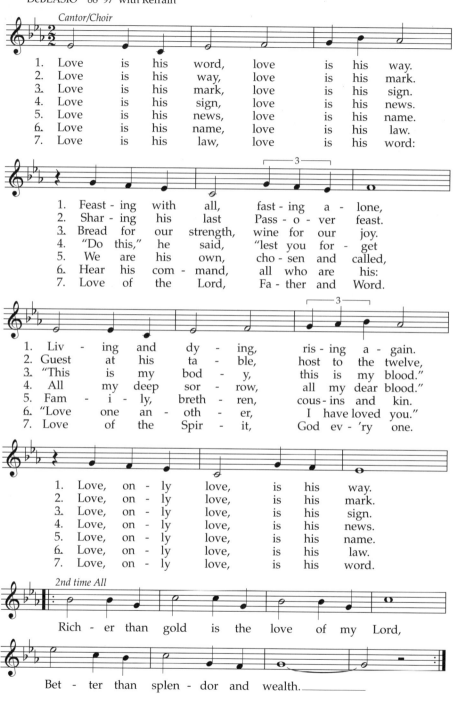

Cantor/Choir

1. Love is his word, love is his way.
2. Love is his way, love is his mark.
3. Love is his mark, love is his sign.
4. Love is his sign, love is his news.
5. Love is his news, love is his name.
6. Love is his name, love is his law.
7. Love is his law, love is his word:

1. Feast - ing with all, fast - ing a - lone,
2. Shar - ing his last Pass - o - ver feast.
3. Bread for our strength, wine for our joy.
4. "Do this," he said, "lest you for - get
5. We are his own, cho - sen and called,
6. Hear his com - mand, all who are his:
7. Love of the Lord, Fa - ther and Word.

1. Liv - ing and dy - ing, ris - ing a - gain.
2. Guest at his ta - ble, host to the twelve,
3. "This is my bod - y, this is my blood."
4. All my deep sor - row, all my dear blood."
5. Fam - i - ly, breth - ren, cous - ins and kin.
6. "Love one an - oth - er, I have loved you."
7. Love of the Spir - it, God ev - 'ry one.

1. Love, on - ly love, is his way.
2. Love, on - ly love, is his mark.
3. Love, on - ly love, is his sign.
4. Love, on - ly love, is his news.
5. Love, on - ly love, is his name.
6. Love, on - ly love, is his law.
7. Love, on - ly love, is his word.

2nd time All

Rich - er than gold is the love of my Lord,

Bet - ter than splen - dor and wealth.

Luke Connaughton, 1917–1979
Text © 1970, McCrimmon Publishing Co., Ltd.

Calvin Hampton, 1938–1984
Music © 1997, WLP

O Cross of Christ

1. O cross of Christ, im - mor - tal tree On
2. From bit - ter death and bar - ren wood The
3. O faith - ful Cross, you stand un - moved While
4. Give glo - ry to the ris - en Christ And

1. which our Sav - ior died, The world is shel - tered
2. tree of life is made; Its branch - es bear un -
3. ag - es run their course: Foun - da - tion of the
4. to his Cross give praise, The sign of God's un -

1. by your arms That bore the Cru - ci - fied.
2. fail - ing fruit And leaves that nev - er fade.
3. u - ni - verse, Cre - a - tion's bind - ing force.
4. fath - omed love, The hope of all our days.

Stanbrook Abbey Hymnal
Text © 1974 Stanbrook Abbey Music

Ananias Davisson's *Kentucky Harmony*, 1816

Send Forth Your Spirit, O Lord

REFRAIN

Send forth your Spir - it, O Lord,_____ and re - new the
face of the earth._____ Send forth your Spir - it, O
Lord, and re - new the face of the earth._____

VERSES

Cantor

1. Bless_____ the Lord,_____ O_____ my soul, Lord
2. Lord,_____ my God,_____ great are your works! In
3. All of your crea - tures look_____ to you, to

1. God,_____ how great you are,_____
2. wis - dom you made them all._____
3. give them their food in time._____ You

1. wrapped in a gar - ment of glo - ry and might,_____
2. Rich is the earth_____ and filled with your life._____
3. give with a - bun-dance, they gath - er it up,_____

To Refrain

1. ___ clothed in light as in_____ a robe._____
2. ___ Bless the Lord, O bless,___ my soul!_____
3. ___ by your hands they have___ their fill._____

Ps 104

Steven C. Warner
Text and music © 1996, WLP

*T*aste and See

Ps 34

James E. Moore, Jr.
Text and music © 1983, GIA

The Sacrament of Service

JEFFERSON   87 87 D

1. Je - sus, Teach - er, Lord and Mas - ter, Af - ter
2. Si - mon Pe - ter said in pro - test: "You shall
3. By our lives and our ex - am - ple, May the

1. eat - ing with his friends, Took a towel and filled a
2. nev - er wash my feet!" "You must let me," said the
3. gos - pel strong-ly speak; Where your chil - dren live in

1. ba - sin, Washed their feet, and then he said: "In re -
2. Sav - ior, "If my king - dom you would see." "Wash me
3. hun - ger, Where the strong op - press the weak. Je - sus,

1. mem-brance, in re - mem-brance, You must do as I___ have
2. clean!" cried Si - mon Pe - ter, "Hands and head as well as
3. grant us un - der-stand - ing Of the sac - ra - ments you

1. done. In re - mem - brance, you must do___ this
2. feet!" Je - sus said: "No, my be - tray - er
3. show; In our sac - ra - ment of serv - ice,

1. For God's daugh - ters and God's sons."
2. Is the one not whol - ly clean."
3. Let us live for oth - ers now.

Alan J. Hommerding
Text © 1996, WLP

The Sacred Harp, Philadelphia, 1844

105

This Joyful Eastertide

VRUECHTEN 67 67 with Refrain

1. This joy - ful Eas - ter - tide, A - way with sin and
2. Death's flood has lost its chill, Since Je - sus crossed the
3. My flesh in hope shall rest, And for a sea - son

1. sor - row! My love, the Cru - ci - fied,
2. riv - er: Great Lord of life, from ill
3. slum - ber, Till trum - pet calls' be - hest

1. Has sprung to life this mor - row.
2. My pass - ing life de - liv - er.
3. Shall wake the dead in num - ber.

Had Christ, who once was slain, ne'er burst his three - day

pris - on, Our faith had been in vain;

But now is Christ a - ris - en, a - ris - en, a -

ris - en, a - ris - en.

George R. Woodward, 1848–1934, alt.

David's Psalmen, Amsterdam, 1686

We Adore You, O Christ

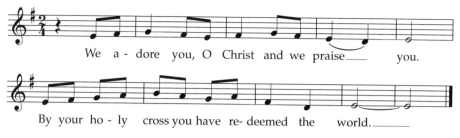

We a - dore you, O Christ and we praise___ you.

By your ho - ly cross you have re- deemed the world.___

Denise Morency Gannon
Music © 1995, WLP

We Remember

We re - mem-ber how you loved us___ to your death,

and still we cel-e-brate, for you are with us here;___

And we be-lieve_ that we will see you___ when you come

in your glo - ry, Lord.___ We re - mem - ber,___ we

cel - e - brate, we be - lieve.___

(380) Marty Haugen
Text and music © 1980, GIA

You Have Put on Christ

You__ have__ put on Christ, in him you have been bap- tized.

Al - le - lu - ia, al - le - lu - ia.

Gal 3:27

Howard L. Hughes
Text and music © 1969, 1977, ICEL

You Will Draw Water Joyfully

You will draw wa - ter joy - ful - ly__ from the

springs of sal - va - tion.

Text © 1969, ICEL

Bob Moore
Music © 1993, WLP

Music Index:
TITLES & FIRST LINES

Title/First Line	Page